M000223175

From
Poverty
—— to ——
Prosperity

A Ghetto Exit Strategy as a Rite of Passage

Charles J. Jones, M.A.

"Jermaine Jones' superb book is a courageous and visionary work that provides concrete steps to overcome white supremacy. Don't miss it!"
- Cornel West

"Mr. Jermaine Jones has written a very compelling and insightful book about some very important areas affecting the lives of too many educationally, economically, and socially disadvantaged people. He brings a fresh eye, first-hand knowledge of and a compassionate understanding to his work. Mr. Jones speaks with authority about some challenging topics, and he provides facts to help make his case. *From Poverty to Prosperity* is a book that should be required reading for all parents and those working in professions that assist young adults. In addition to offering you different ways of seeing the challenges, it will also give you a new language and some new tools for addressing them."

Dr. Wilbur Brower,
author of Me Teacher, Me Please!!

"In a time of severe crisis that threatens the very existence of the Black Male in America - comes a powerful message to inspire youth and men to change the way they think about IMAGE, Prosperity, Identity and Self-Confidence in themselves... Jermaine Jones brings a sign of hope and reality in a power packed book. A must read for the African American Community."

Tyrone Holmes
Founder & CEO
The Men of Semper Fidelis, Inc.

"Jermaine Jones has released an interesting critique of the pathologies plaguing the African American community. However, only when these pathologies are viewed against the backdrop of the cause, historical global white supremacy, can we move from diagnosis to cure."

Paul Scott, NoWarningShotsFired.com

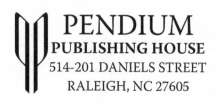

PENDIUM
PUBLISHING HOUSE
514-201 DANIELS STREET
RALEIGH, NC 27605

For information, please visit our Web site at
www.pendiumpublishing.com

PENDIUM Publishing and its logo
are registered trademarks.

FROM POVERTY TO PROSPERITY
A GHETTO EXIT STRATEGY AS A RITE OF PASSAGE
By Charles J. Jones, M.A.

ISBN: 978-1-936513-56-7

PUBLISHER'S NOTE

This book is printed on acid-free paper.

On behalf of Jamaal Griggs, Al Jones, Travian Mitchell, Mark English, Brian Murphy, Cimarron Reed, Malcolm Reed, John Sloan, Keith Sumpter, Jonathan Brunson, Rod Williams, Quincy Wright, Greg Bellamy, Leon Washington, and Phil Gowins, all are men who have committed themselves to strengthening the *black* community through spirituality, education, or self-motivation. You brothers are all imperative and commended for your efforts in not only trying to save the *black* community, but above all, the *black* race. Continue to encourage *black* men and women to refuse to animate the handwringing typecasts which hauntingly shadow us, as well as champion those who social order has calculatingly disregarded.

Acknowledgments

My intense contentment goes first and foremost to the Messiah, Jesus Christ. I am fully aware that without Him nothing is possible, but with Him, all is. Even when those around me disregarded, did not, and refused to see my vision in writing this book, He kept my view clear. Too, in regards to God's refinement, despite every negative deliberation which attempted to persuade me to not complete this book, false accusations strapped to fiery arrows, immunizations of malevolence, and emotive opportunities which bent my faith to curvature limits and made an effort to persuade me to throw in the towel—they all fell to the ground before affronting me.

As well, I am grateful for Bishop Melvin G. Brown, Pastor of Greater New Hope Baptist Church in N.W. Washington, D.C., for being such a vigorous vessel of God and keeping me spiritually adjusted throughout the process of completing this tome.

The entire Jones family; my mother Rose; my sister Jackie—this generation's Harriet Tubman—J.B.; Tim Jr.; Javion; and my brothers Tim and James are this book's pillars. The support from you all throughout the course of completing this manuscript has been unprecedented. James, thank you for redefining the term 'Warrior' and what it really means to be a sound provider. Tim, thank you for revealing to me at a very early age how important it is for

7

one to obtain a sound education, primarily *blacks*, and that the act of one becoming educated extends far beyond any classroom. Peace to the both of you.

Dr. Ogede, my former professor of English Studies at North Carolina Central University, provided his valuable time and imperative and pedagogic guidance during decisive phases of this project. I remain heavily in his debt. Too, Ms. Lili Pollock and Dr. Cornel West at Princeton University contributed to this project in a manner that could have only been predetermined by God. I can't thank you two enough.

Lisa Shea assisted me in the premature stages of this project. Her wisdom and advice were both paramount.

As well, I would like to express thanks to Leah Gordon, my publicist, for her generosity, great ideas, and genuine concern for my intentions in writing this book. Rod Walton, Renee Stevens, Josephine Kerr, and Chenita Rountree, all who are not only great friends, but also great people, provided unlimited support and assistance when I faced robust obstacles, performed research, and pressed to complete this project. Their integrity is everlasting. As well, I am grateful for the robust exchange of ideas I was able to engage in with my barber Anthony (A.B.) Barnes, Lashon Harley, Kevin Pettiford, Tarica Rawlinson, Alton Taybron, Qentin Rogers, Alterick Gastons, Tiyati Speight, Keta Newborn, Brandon Wellington, Tyrone Wellington, and Cory Best.

Sherina Johnson imparted more than she can imagine, extended her generosity, and assisted in various manners.

As well, I am indebted to Rhonda Deans for her challenging perspectives which defied me to redefine my intentions for inscribing this book. Rhonda, thank you.

Too, I would like to salute Edward Arnold and the entire Pendium Publishing organization. Your professionalism and authentic concern for this project cannot be measured. Edward, thanks for your patience and issuing me sound advice even when my agenda inconvenienced yours.

I owe as well to the countless number of foreign students who I had the pleasure of edifying. In particular, Amirasah Bah, Marie Hiller, and Grace Rowsey, who are all from West Africa. They allocated their personal experiences and passions to learn with me. In addition, these students provided the essence of this text.

Correspondingly, I indisputably express gratitude to Nasir "Nas" Jones for providing me with the soundtrack to this manuscript via his anthologies of verbal sonatas which, too, address the plights, internally and externally, *blacks* must elude in order to survive America.

Ultimately, I express gratefulness to the scores of *black* men and women who allowed me into their personal worlds and have genuinely decided to seek the *From Poverty to Prosperity* experience. You all are the reason for me writing this book. Lastly, as with anything that I inscribe, I accept full responsibility for any of this manuscript's shortcomings.

To be born a black male in America is to be put into shackles and then challenged to escape. Those shackles are as daunting as any faced by Houdini. But just as the handcuffs, the prisons cells, even the coffins that confined Houdini eventually bent to his wall, the chains that bind us will yield as well, provided that we attack them shrewdly.

Ellis Cose,

BLACK HIM

Married to the residue of America's streets
Unaware of his potential
Only if being tuff was the remedy to his problems
Only if being tuff was the panacea to solve them
He could then defeat the one bully that torments him daily
(Self-Doubt)
Then life would be much easier for the brother
Manufactured from a fatherless home

BLACK HER

Since a lass, she's been devoid of diplomacy
Since forever, daddie was miss'n and mommie wasn't
list'nen
Now she permanently hides behind an invisible curt'n
Some thought it was her feelings
But it was her soul hurt'n
A loose heart hiding behind tight clothes
Hoping men notice her

JERMAINE JONES

Preface
By The Author

In terms of surviving America, what exactly does that mean for *black* people today? We could begin, cognitively, diagnosing this question by first reading the subtle inscriptions which have been emotively engraved within a very distinctive diary chronicled by history—a memoir which suffers from unending internal bleeding and meticulously documents *black* life here in America. The lettering within this memoir is heavily tinged with the likes of crimson and bears witness to the perpetual and numerous assaults on the *black* race as an entirety via the slave trade—slave labor; Jim Crow laws—incalculable lynchings; vicious ideologies of white colonization—white supremacy; and the unremitting psychological duping by whites which trained *blacks* to systematically hate themselves, emotionally marry materialistic items, feel affection for physical violence, reject methods of prosperity which require the use of cognitive muscle, abode fear, and cling to victimization for the purpose of dominating their intelligence. So then, consequently, for *blacks* living within America today, the underlying litmus conformities which award them social equality: education, citizenship, sound occupations, government assistance, laws, affirmative typecasts, and financial likelihoods have somehow, decade after decade, found a vigorous approach to become deviously inverted as these same egalitarianisms have worked in opposition, lambasted, and relinquished all protection for people of color. Now, with that being highlighted, what does the term surviving America mean in regards to *black* people?

Despite the obvious, in terms of race related setbacks which are, of course, still daunting obstacles for *blacks* to contend with, I believe right now is the best time to be *black* since our existence in this country. There are, today, more opportunities for us to become whatever it is we want to without having to mask our dreams and aspirations— something our forerunners had to do incessantly out of trepidation. Never has there been an epoch in our history where it was uncomplicated to find a vast number of *blacks* owing their own businesses, obtaining multiple degrees, not yet breaking, but persistently puncturing glass ceilings, steam heading the political arena, and dominating sports, that for years, whites governed.

Although bigotry is very much animated and still subsist within America today, *blacks*, via our accomplishments and astute campaigns which candidly confront and exploit the weaknesses of America's political defensive strategies, have attacked racism and overt outlines of discrimination in a manner that has forced them to, at least, bend to their curvature limits.

Albeit, a vast number of *blacks* are still finding it therapeutic to ignore the fine print our unsmiling history has chronicled, fine print which provides detailed attestation why we *must* acquire the necessary tools of survival in America, and perpetually practice self-sedating customs and norms. This is only confirmation that *blacks*, after such a protracted time frame of digesting America's nauseating suggestions for their well-being—false self-fulfilling prophesies (false information) disguised as winning strate-gies—have become inherently queasy while simultaneously authorizing their personal worlds—deadly metropolitan avenues, the "hood", gangsta rap music, the idea of victim-ization, "authentic" *blackness*, chauvinism, and negative media typecasts—to initiate a new behavior, resulting in false information becoming true. This action, also known as *"The Pygmalion Effect"*, suggests that such an accomplish-ment prompts inferior thinkers to live up to the expecta-tions of those of authority. For some confounding reason, *black* people have become motivated to conduct themselves in a manner that suggest they will be better off doing exactly what is expected of them, particularly if the behaviors are down beat, self-sedating, impair them to the point of no return, and yield dire consequences.

Thus, my topmost premise for authoring this book is to conscientiously address and attempt to counter that deleterious effect. Understand however, with any catch—22, in order for one to genuinely resolve it, or at least attempt to, all of the problematic apprehensions that lead up to the entrapment must be clearly highlighted, first. Establishing that point, throughout this entire book, I highlight and explore some of the most damaging and self-sedating stings that have shaped *blacks'* practices here in America—practices they are executing relentlessly with the intentions of surviving America, but will never yield any affluent results. And of course these very practices are customs that America has purposely repudiated and have no merit beyond the citadels of the "hood" and metropolitan avenues.

So then, you can regard this manuscript as your very own self-effacing *Jones' Free At Last Kit, Culprit Identifier,* or *Self-imprisonment Key* to assist in your navigation through unchartered territory imbued with landmines of daunting internal and external enigmas as you shadow opulence here in America. Subsequent to affixing yourself to the particularized title that fits your liking, I suggest, strongly, that you read this manuscript in its entirety with diligence and the anticipation of transitioning from *Poverty to Prosperity.*

Contents

Introduction: Machinate

INTRODUCTION

MACHINATE

If one were to systematically examine history, it would be effortless finding evidence proving that America, more so its generations and eras, approved demons which attempted to asphyxiate the existence of the *black* race from the foundation of its social scale to its apex. From the horrendous events of slavery 400 plus years ago; to bigotry and the malevolence of the KKK in the 30's, 40's, and 50's; to the fight for social equality and being relegated to the status of substandard citizens under Jim Crow laws from the 1800's to the 1960's; to the AIDS and crack epidemics throughout the 80's and 90's; and more recently, the malicious military weather patterns and natural disasters which have been progressively rumored to be controlled and manipulated by manufactured devices to kill off *blacks*, we have endured more hardships than any other minority race this country has ever welcomed without any intermissions. I often contemplate if some of the enigmas which have been a lethal force on the face of this earth were intentionally structured within a surreptitious affirmation, by the powers that be, to purposely seek and destroy *blacks*. And for all, regardless of skin color, who feel that this hypothesis was or is currently one of validity, they would probably agree that it intimately bears a resemblance to the following:

19

THE OFFICIAL 4 STEP AFFIRMATION TO DESTROY THE BLACK RACE

- *STEP 1: Procure all of the blacks who are uneducated and jobless, and disconnect them away from the select minority who just so happen to exceed America's expectations. As well, disengage the uneducated away from all aspects of obtaining education and independent thinking, so that they will remain easily manipulated, unmotivated, emotionally distorted, and psychologically suppressed. Doing this will create multiple low-income environments to target and make it easier to convince blacks that they are not suppose to be successful nor educated and those who are should be considered "Uncle Toms".*

- *STEP 2: Continue to implement racism, addiction, and the ideology of slavery into the lives of blacks, but in antithetic forms and fashions. Filter this corruption through institutions such as banks, schools, government, record labels, computer based networking websites (Facebook & dating sources), T.V. programs, and laws.*

- *STEP 3: Take advantage of these afflicted people by introducing them to methods that will help them cope with their state of being. Instead of education, counseling, and financial relief, give them crack, cancer, large doses of T.V. diversions, AIDS (a man made virus), guns, gangsta rap, and everything off-putting that only this particular group of people will be able to relate to. Make them believe that this way of life is normal and calculatingly allow a few from this population to prosper from drug profits, number running, and other forms of hustling to make other blacks envy them and soon plot to kill. This should be the final ingredient to the results we are looking for.*

- *STEP 4: At last, place all of these blacks in a box together, on one side of town, (in the projects, low-income housing, and impoverished localities without zoning policies) and close the lid. We can open it once every two weeks to take out all of the dead bodies. In about 10 to 15 years, the black race should be on the path of extinction.*

Even if you have never been one to accord thought to conspiracy theories, you must admit that these events certainly mirror what has occurred throughout the history of America and are by far the most cynical measures which have navigated their way into *black* communities since their existence. As a complete race, we would love to believe that this plan is inaccurate, but if one were to extract various racial testimonies and acts away from America's pockets, it would appear as if the *black* race has been in line for a scheduled execution for a very long time. Despite the probable man-made demons that have haunted *blacks* in America, many have discovered an effective and clear-cut method to avoid them while, simultaneously, navigating thoroughly through the unjust smog in which this great country has to offer by investigating various outlets that authorized them to become a living success. I'm grateful to see that many of us have excelled in entertainment, education, athletics, entrepreneurship, and many other arenas; however, a large number of *blacks* were not so lucky.

While a sensible number of *blacks* have been able to escape poverty, there are a massive number of brothers and sisters who have found themselves wedged at the bottom of America's socio-economic ladder. Those who fit into this category make up the majority of uneducated and low-income *blacks* who took a path that was neither promising nor beneficial in order for them to become successful. For others, unfortunate circumstances landed them where they are. Regardless of the motives, I firmly believe if one wants to become a better asset within society, it is exceedingly possible and never too late to do so.

I would like to initiate my oration via a few strong declarations. First, I would like to acknowledge and highlight the fact that *blacks* who make up low-income populations are neither obtuse nor unteachable; these brothers and sisters are just simply unaware of the potential they possess and have failed to obtain and tap into the necessary skills that will grant them authorization to operate free from governmental dependency within this world of institutional racism and gender bias. As a result of their ill-fated circumstances, this population is very closely monitored by America's restrictions and exceedingly limited to what they can and cannot do, which altogether places them at a huge disadvantage to those who reside on the opposite end of the emancipation spectrum within American society. Financial and didactic limitations, poverty, and many other hardships have forced a good number of this population to adapt attitudes of hatred and anger towards themselves, society, and even middle class *blacks*. Even though, I would like for all of my brothers and sisters, no matter if you are educated, uneducated, wealthy or living in poverty, to genuinely understand that time has expired for us to continue opting for silence and ignoring the self-inflicted and crippling issues which are plaguing *blacks* as well as *black* communities across the United States.

Blacks for some conspicuous reason, in particular high-profile *blacks*—those who possess the social leverage to bring issues plaguing *black* communities above a whisper— don't speak candidly about these anxieties, because they fear looking dreadful, fear their cultural PR will be ruined, fear what white America may assume of them, or fear *blacks* will indict them for applying counter-racism to an unprivileged population. We can no longer remain silent and ignore our community's self-inflicted wounds out of fear. Refusing to honestly and diligently deliberate all of the issues which are paralyzing and tearing *black* communities apart will only promise us that all of these issues will remain unanswered.

In my second declaration, I would like to vigorously encourage readers not to panic. This manuscript is not another tome that situates all of the apprehensions within the *black* race at the feet of America while simultaneously blaming the "white man" for the personal obstructions, lack of motivation, self-defeated attitudes, and financial defi-

ciencies of *blacks* who are victims of less fortunate circumstances. Mentioning that, do not misconstrue my message here either. I am not, under any circumstance, attempting to paint an insincere picture that down plays racism in America, nor am I trying to superficially deduct its power, because although racism or what I refer to as (the slash) did not physically place *blacks* in housing projects, government welfare lines, poor rundown neighborhoods, and poverty—stricken living conditions, it did indeed establish these horrific circumstances with the intentions of them all perpetually remaining a generational consuming whirlwind for us to contend with as well as dominate us—all because we (*blacks*) were never invited to co-exist within society along with our counter-parts. In the book *Isis Papers*, Dr. Frances C. Welsing elaborated on this same premise and explained what she believed to be a vehicle for racism when she wrote:

> **Racism evolved with the singular goal of white supremacy or white power domination by the global white minority over the vast non-white global majority. This colored global collective has been forced into the position of relative powerlessness compared to the global white collective establishing the power equation of white over non-white (W/N-W).**

The intentions of this rigorous social segregation, or better yet white power domination, has somehow found a way, decade after decade in a very inconspicuous manner, to continuously carry out what it was conceived to do.

Let's just be honest here, one of the many malevolent goals of racial discrimination (the slash), from the initiation of slavery, was and still is to socially exclude *blacks* away from white American society. As a result of this malevolence, America's ghettos have become the overflow rooms for *blacks* who do not outlive this country's rejection. Dr. Stephen Steinberg, a sociologist, distinguished Professor at the University of California-Berkeley, and author on race and ethnicity in the United States wrote in his book, *The Ethnic Myth*, "Ghettos are nothing less than the shameful residue of slavery." In fact, evidence proving that racism and its power, especially tactical racism (a cunning method to apply racism unseen on radar), are very much vivacious today can be found in the following four monumental cases that recently occurred right under America's nose:

CASE #1 HURRICANE KATRINA

The 2005 hurricane Katrina catastrophe exposed the veiled slash within America as well as her assumption

on the topic of racism. The events surrounding Hurricane Katrina offered a remarkable case study of the social divide in the United States. It was no secret that the residents most affected by the results

of this proclaimed natural disaster were *blacks* who all met the guidelines of living in poverty. Although initially ignored, chiefly by the media, the racial aspects (the slash) of this tragedy were resurrected the moment rapper Kanye West blatantly declared on national T.V., "George Bush doesn't care about *black* people." His comment was a result of the government not acting in a timely fashion to transport supplies, food, and life saving medical care to the devastated area. As a result, thousands died, the crime rate sky rocketed, and all of the victims affected by this disaster found themselves homeless. West's comment brewed an inferno, because although we were unable to see racism through the spectacles of bigotry and hooded sheets, it was clear that tactical racism was indeed in full effect and being heavily applied to this event via the positions of power by means of social exclusion. A defense apparatus within this country, one that whites unremittingly color themselves with to avoid being viewed as racist, is the fact that America is the land of opportunity; therefore, why are people not taking advantage of the many avenues that are available to avoid poverty? Although moderately true, it's hard to make up lost ground when our prime opponents started on their debris free paths to prosperity yesterday, while our paths have been laced with hazardous ruins. Mentioning that, Katrina victims who were forced to leave couldn't afford to come back to what they knew as home, because the expensive rebuilding process forced all of those poverty-stricken *blacks* out. This tragedy provided *black* America with unprecedented proof that racism is not only a substance of psychological hatred, but of political and economic prohibiting as well. The cold hard fact is that most of white-America, in particular the Presidential administration active during the hurricane Katrina tragedy, did not regard the victims as wholly belonging to the same society they lived in.

CASE #2 THE JENA SIX INCIDENT

As well, in 2007, old-fashion plantation racism instituted its way back into the face of 20th century *black* America when six young *black* males from Jena, Louisiana were looking at twenty plus years in prison in a clear case of modern day "Jim Crow" justice. This story of racial injustice was inaugurated when a noose hanging prank, pulled by white students, was carried out after *black* students sat under, what was considered to be, an all "Whites Tree". After making a visit to the site where the incident took place, the DA, who was white, found it necessary to dismiss the noose incident as only a "prank". This move by the DA was one that was very

much connected to the preceding reality that our ancestors faced, one in which *blacks* today would rather forget. Consequently, this sparked several series of white on *black* incidents leaving six *black* students facing insensitive jail time for the beating of a white student who had addressed several *black* students as "Niggers" and taunted a *black* student who was beaten up prior at a party away from school. This same white student found himself on the wrong end of a school yard brawl after eating lunch at school, and this particular event ignited racial tensions that were fueled by hate. These six young *black* men, as well as their families, had more than enough reasons to have feared for their lives daily. There was even an account when the six *black* students were threatened by a white gentleman who drew a gun on them. Feeling that their lives were in danger, these young students vigorously disarmed the gentleman without anyone getting hurt, and as a result, the white man ran off. Even though authorities were aware of the white gentlemen drawing the gun on the *black* students, no charges were ever brought against him, but the *black* students were arrested and charged with gun theft. This story mirrors those exactly from the era of Jim Crow existence. Within this case, the judge, jurors, and lawyers were all white and made a robust attempt to use the justice system to bully and prove to these *blacks* who possessed power.

CASE #3 THE MRS. SHIRLEY SHERROD FIRING

Again in 2010, racism levitated and fueled a story of failed research and redemption involving Mrs. Shirley Sherrod, a *black* former Rural Development USDA secretary who was wrongfully fired. In an attempt to personally attack Mrs. Sherrod and not the NAACP, a white blogger and also Tea Party member by the name of Andrew Briethart released an edited and doctored up two minute tape that was repeatedly ran in a loop by *Fox News* of an oration that Mrs. Sherrod gave years prior.

This brief clip was used to falsely accuse her of verbally exercising racial discrimination amongst white farmers, when in actuality, the unedited and authentic oration displayed Mrs. Sherrod making an effort to lead the coalition in a direction that would allow them to begin to overcome their race related issues. Instead of displaying due diligence first, the media as well as the government

 assumed the tape depicted an accurate account of her character and immediately abandoned Mrs. Sherrod without contacting her personally. They both just threw her under the bus, not knowing all of the facts.

Andrew Briethart and the media were trusting that the video would prove Mrs. Sherrod to indeed be a racist, so that her character would soon be obtainable for assassination, while in actuality they both were cunningly exercising racism themselves. This case confirmed that racism (the slash) is very vivacious and ready to be exercised and fired in the direction of the *black* race as a stern reminder of who ultimately has the power in the United States of America.

There were two shocking phenomenon which were highlighted within this particular case. **1)** The fact that the White House was so easily duped by this forged footage from an individual who was not even a journalist and had no journalism credentials. **2)** How quickly and influential the reckless action of Andrew Briethart, a man with a history of smeared campaigning, was able to rally the world of viral politics and force the government, expeditiously, into making an irrational decision to reprimand Mrs. Sherrod without researching the event for clarity first. Was this speedy and unconstructive response executed without seeking the truth, first, primarily because the White House bleeds white votes? It wasn't until the NAACP decided to investigate, review, and rerelease the entire tape that the truth was able to be unveiled.

*CASE #4 Blacks **And Their Voting Rights***

A newly registered voter in Selma, Alabama, in August 1965

This picture is excerpted from the book Free At Last: The U.S. Civil Rights Movement, published by the Bureau of International Information Programs.

The Voting Rights Act of 1965 was one of the most monumental victories for *blacks* collectively here in the United States of America in terms of obtaining civil rights and being able to assert ourselves as permanent participants in a democratic system. Despite this great victory, today, we still have not hurdled all of the deceitful voting contingencies that threaten the integrity of our votes and quietly hinder us from completely obtaining the freedom we are entitled to within voting booths. Although the 15th Amendment to the Constitution of the United States prohibits federal or state governments from infringing on a citizen's right to vote on account of race, color, or previous condition of servitude, it's a disgrace that *blacks*, in 2012, have to depend on the renewal of the Voting Rights Act of 1965 in order to be able to vote without the threat of discriminatory voting practices occurring. This Act has been renewed and extended by Congress four times in order to authorize the government to oversee voting practices in most Southern states. The most recent renewed 25-year extension was signed into law by George W. Bush in 2006.

Despite the vivacious presence of racism and its task to continue to exercise misogyny against *blacks* in this country as well as its strongholds, I simply would like for all of my brothers and sisters to understand that racism will forever be a feature in our lives as long as we remain *black*, but we can no longer perceive it as a *black* cloud in which we don't have the ability to evade, even tactical racism (racism unseen on radar) and its powers. Even so, always understand that it is not the punch you see, but the punch you don't see that will knock you out.

It's becoming extremely common, today, for *blacks* to become so beat down from daily existence and hurdling the hindrances from the corridors we have opted to take in our lives that we just spiritually, mentally, and physically collapse, while crediting our defeat to white America reserving their right to exercise racism against us. Therefore, instead of placing blame at the feet of our counter-parts, my aim here is more self-effacing as I address what we, *blacks* living within America, need to do as a race and individually in order to transition from *Poverty to Prosperity*.

One major goal of mine in writing this book is to not only extend myself to and uplift *blacks* who are components of America's low-income populations, but all *blacks* who are cradled within their self-crafted revulsions and hopefully help them find a sense of self-worth and motivation through various avenues of enlightenment. But in doing so, I *must* candidly point out and highlight some of the most damaging actions that we (*blacks*) are continuing to execute on a daily basis that have us paralyzed in our self-created worlds. Also, I will explore a minority of the government's ongoing regulations and strongholds that continue to weigh heavy on low-income *blacks* and restrain the masses within this population. Ultimately, my reach is to provide *blacks* who find themselves exchanging blows, on a daily basis, with America's purposely premeditated threats—threats which are designed specifically for our race—with a tangible escape route away from governmental dependency by sharing obtainable strategies that will allow them to genuinely believe in themselves and tap into their unused potential.

Let me be unmistakably clear here. In order for you to transition from *Poverty to Prosperity*, you must first understand that it is definitely going to take faith, focus, strategic planning, and intense sacrifice amongst other things. This will initially be a rigid task to perform, particularly when you have been advised all of your life to lower your sights while simultaneously living within conditions that have, cognitively, conditioned you to accept your destitute lifestyle, one that's far from prosperous, as a conventional method of living. Too, you must understand that I am not advancing some distinguished panacea that will majestically consent to America's anonymous and less fortunate populations becoming filthy rich overnight. The truth is, it's not that simple.

Mentioning that, also understand that the transition in which I am promoting does not abruptly end with you brothers and sisters changing your monetary state of being only; it also incorporates you modifying your current spiritual, educational, and mental position as well. I strongly believe that if you would reconstruct your entire method of thinking, it would be much easier for you to confront your self-worth and detach yourselves away from living the life society expects you all to live. I love my culture and race dearly, and will defend them both extensively, but I also do not have a problem, at all, condemning either of them when they are wrong for the sake of motivating them.

Through faith and sacrifice my family and I were able to break down poverty's wall and escape its ideological customs and norms. Therefore, because I am a product of the same environment that I am diligently reaching out to, I have the right and a chief obligation to light a fire beneath my people. I have even more of an obligation to point out all of the negative entities that we are continually engaging in. As well, I have the right to be affronted by each brother and sister who believed everyone who told them they would never amount to anything; however, I too understand the many horrifying issues that this population encounters on a daily basis and how these issues can lead to many of them developing self-defeating attitudes. More importantly, I understand why this population feels as though they are on an island alone and no longer have anything in common with middle class *blacks*. Most *black* men and women in low-income localities only role models were their fathers, but unfortunately for almost all of them, those relationships were cut short. In a number of cases, the lack of love and support from their fathers, especially those without older brothers, forced *blacks* within America's metropolitan city limits to permanently carry a burden of abandonment and seek life lessons from forged relationships, the streets, and its cruel activities.

As a man, the feelings that are conceived from being disowned by his father carry a pain that cuts deep within the soul and will leave a permanent scar. Many men won't admit this, but the emotional pain they bear from the absence of their biological fathers has altered their social interaction, especially with women. And for *black* women, the affects of an absent father is even more agonizing. Some view their fathers, the one male that they are suppose to be able to trust perpetually, as the first man who abandoned them and broke their hearts.

Experiencing this pain, in addition to watching their single mothers reach an apex of stress from just trying to survive day to day, have persuaded a large number of *black* women to elude taking a path to success, and regrettably, most have never found a way to rebound from that unfortunate decision. Consequently, they have gone searching for love from older men, become sexually active at a very early age, and accepted abuse, mental and physical, early in their lives. Mentioning abuse, for some *black* women, their self-defeated attitudes have been shaped by the effects of molestation by their mother's boyfriend or worse, a family member, which has altered their views of their own self-worth as well as *black* men. Some are even treating their own male children unjust, because a man sexually abused them. Though damaging, I am not campaigning that these issues articulate that *blacks* who are raised in a single parent home will not eventually turn out to be successful or ever triumph. Actually, a good number of *blacks* who have emerged from single parent homes are doing quite well. The point I would like to make here is that in a large number of cases, the absence of a parent, *black* fathers more specifically, can very well be one of the multiple factors that contribute to a child obtaining a self-defeated attitude as they mature into adulthood.

These issues are just a few tear drops in the bucket that have plagued poverty stricken *blacks*. This assessment omits the wide range of drug and alcohol abuse as means of therapeutic ejection, depression, and feelings of helplessness that have touched almost everyone within this population. Suffocating matters such as these have this populace on the ground in a crouching position and are continuously kicking them and will continue to kick them if they allow it to happen. Again, I empathize for these brothers and sisters, but I do not condone the fact that they have just completely relinquished their right to trade punches with self-defeat and given up. I understand clearly that these are some major setbacks attached to very heavy emotional strains that most have encountered, but one must come to terms with seeking help in order to positively move through life.

To begin this journey, I strongly suggest to those who are truly searching to make a life changing transition to begin seeking spiritual strengthening and emotional empowering first and foremost. You would be exceedingly surprised by the countless avenues of help that are available through a genuine church community.

True, we are very strong people, but emotional strains are even stronger. For some strange reason the dominance of *black* men and women, more so *black* men, has always been partnered with corporeal strength. Loud, strong, and demanding tones when we are speaking, plus bullying facial expressions, have been considered some of the most coercing weapons that *black* people possess. In the past, mainly via movies and written scribes, these traits seemed to have over ridden the artistic and academic accomplishments of *blacks* which are less celebrated. History as well as society has done such an immense job of tattooing this notion into the minds of *blacks*, that at one point, we almost believed that the only way we could exist within the presence of success in America was to fit into the ball player, MC, floozy, or drug dealer category—especially throughout the 80's and 90's. Thank God we have transitioned to an epoch where it is undemanding to unearth multitudes of positive triumphs about *blacks* to rejoice over, honor, and be proud of.

Regardless of the residue of prejudice that still remains evident and continuously stains America's soil today, I believe that we (*blacks*) have vigilantly gotten the attention of whites as well as every other race existing within this country and exemplified strength in vast areas, that for a protracted amount of time, seemed to be predominately dominated by whites: academics, golf, tennis, and politics just to name a few. We have done this in a manner in which exterior races even agree that we (*blacks*) have and will continue to set trends. This enlightenment is not at all a taunt, but more so a mobilized respective that positions our success, as a race, on a global stage. The hazardous path that *blacks* have been forced to take, every since we took our first steps in this country, makes all of our victories and accomplishments, despite the level they may be on, that much sweeter to rejoice over. This is sound verification why *blacks* have to find delight in fellow brothers and sisters progressing and experiencing success today. As a race, we can no longer purposely place daunting obstacles in the path of our brethren or envy them simply, because they are transitioning to, currently occupying, or have explored an area of little variation we have yet to investigate. If anything, their ability to excel should be solid evidence that proves hard work yields prosperous results for anyone who is willing to sacrifice.

Let's not forget that our ancestors were not considered to be human beings during the course of slavery, but built the White House with their bare hands without prerogative while being consistently overseen by slave holders. Indubitable evidence of this can be found in the book entitled *The Black History of the White House*, authored by Clarence Lusane. Within this book, Mr. Lusane allotted an all-inclusive history of the White House from a slave's perspective. As well, he provided factual stories of enslaved *blacks* who were forced to work on the construction of the mansion at 1600 Pennsylvania Avenue. The following is an excerpt from the book:

> **But these *black* men may have thought themselves more fortunate than others who were forced to slave in extreme conditions at the various slave quarries in and around Virginia. These locations have been described as "snake-infested" and "swarmed with mos-**

quitoes," and the labor so arduous that each worker was given "a half-pint of whisky per day to help them cope." This was a spirit-killing work if such there ever was. Enslaved *black* men were ordered into the quarries from "can't see" to "can't see" to carry out the back-breaking tasks of digging, cutting, lifting, and hauling stone. Tons of the stone from which the U.S. Capital is built, and which can still be seen today, got there via the slave labor of *black* men.

Jesse Holland, as well, within his well-researched book entitled *Black Men built the Capitol*, provided information that dims the standard stories about Washington and shines a light on the labor African American slaves relinquished to the White House, Capitol, and multiple historic structures. Holland wrote:

> The Capitol would not exist as we know it today without slave craftsmanship and labor. Records show that slaves who lived in the Washington, D.C., area made up a good portion of the labor pool that worked on the Capitol. More than four hundred slaves, or more than half of the documented work force that constructed the Capitol, cleared trees from Jenkins Hill and dug up stumps for the wide avenues that radiate out into the city, according to research first publicized by *NBC* reporter Edward Hotaling in 2000.

At present, in 2012, a *black* family has complete authorization of the White House as overseers, along with presiding jurisdiction over the entire world. Let's diligently think about this feat for a minute. Albeit you are one who believes the entire presidential election was fixed, or President Barack Obama is just taking on a role to be the scapegoat for future underlying political catastrophes, your heart has to weep for all of those who died paving the road that lead to this breathtaking accomplishment. Again, I'm not boasting here, nor am I attempting to piggy back on the civil rights movement. I am only using this monumental event to highlight the fact that *black* people can accomplish anything in this country no matter what the task. I doubt if there are many *blacks* in America today, no matter if they are rich, poor, politically inclined or not, educated or uneducated, who genuinely hate the fact the 44th President of the United States is a *black* man who, at one point in his professional career, was also a highly successful attorney as well, regardless of how they feel about his presidential policies. So, why then are *blacks* continually pulling down and envious of the success of their own family members, friends, and in some cases, their own children? As a complete race, all of our accomplishments in this country are ground breaking feats.

Being a prominent minority in this country, we must begin to recognize the magnitude of our historical journey up until this point, examine ourselves individually, and allow other's feats to be a catalyst for our own self-improvement. It is imperative that we continue to expand our excellence as a race in unexpected areas. *Blacks*, particularly those within low-income environments, are not moving in the direction that is conducive for social production.

Blacks today, despite their age, who are successful have at some point in their lives recognized that they were free to elude all of society's visible and invisible strongholds and able to go places and accomplish feats our forerunners had never dreamed of exploring and completing. Oh, and I also must note that a good number of *blacks,* today, who have achieved, are successful, and relinquished their right to query their own abilities not only worked extremely hard to get where they're currently situated, but are also products of poverty and single family homes. If only *blacks* who are products of low-income areas across America would come to terms with their self-worth and the potential they possess to do anything they want to do, so that these brothers and sisters can immediately find their particular path to prosperity instead of continually sinking.

1

POVERTY HAS NO NEIGHBORS

In my many visits to various project housing town hall meetings, I have an opportunity to speak directly to the residents who occupy the government issued units—those who have, to some extent, decided that they want to improve their current living conditions. These are meetings organized by community leaders who are reaching out to individuals from low-income areas to expose them to information regarding furthering their education, strengthening their health, crime prevention, and home ownership minus the government scrutiny. Initially, each of these meetings are all quasi-counterintuitive environments in which the significance of quality living, self-importance, and education are severely undermined—environments where success is failure. For someone who is a product of this environment, this unpleasantness is a bit easier to digest; but for those who are products of a more fortunate upbringing, they would easily be met with cognitive bemusement. While conversing with residents in the first meeting I ever attended, I was able to see, reliably, that self-motivation, hope, and ambition were not, at all, in the repertoire of those who were in attendance. I also got the notion that for a long time, those particular brothers and sisters had solemnly questioned their own abilities, continually relived their dark past, and over time became paralyzed by self-doubt. Even though, the more I was able to gain the trust of those brothers and sisters in attendance, the more they voluntarily opened up to me and revealed their justifications for not progressing in life.

One admitted truth that struck me with anger was that many feared maximizing their potential and illustrating examples of the positive personifications *blacks* are capable of embodying, primarily, because of pressure applied upon them from those within their personal worlds. They feared that pursing success and improving their current living statuses would demolish the bridge that mended them to their community, family, and friends. One resident stated," My friends was already jealous of me, but when I was taking classes they were telling people I think I'm better than them." This particular incident underscored that case after case, householders within this particular population followed this same pattern. As well, it was confirmation to me that *blacks* within low-income localities are actually honoring the "hood" and placing all of its politics on a pedestal. They would rather suffer, significantly, for the sake of satisfying a group of miserable and dependent individuals whose aspirations will never swell than to cut ties with this population and begin seeking prosperity. Even though the attendance at this particular meeting was not filled to capacity, I got a sense that these particular brothers and sisters in attendance were sincerely fed up with their current living conditions and ready to begin a new chapter of their lives which included self-motivation and an immediate detachment from their past. I remember fervently wishing that every individual within every housing project and low-income locality who is summoned to America's rejection would suddenly experience this same emotional metamorphosis that this particular group embraced.

Minutes into the meeting, the few individuals who were in attendance voiced that they had enough of living in poverty, relying on government assistance, and admitted that their slothful methods of living compelled them to envy *blacks* who had labored callously and were reaping the benefits of their labor. It was if this particular meeting was therapeutic and they took on the responsibility of being spokespersons for every "hood" in America. In addition to the facilitators giving them information that could possibly help them gain leverage over their current living conditions, I told this group that if they would just unchain their minds and hearts and distance themselves away from negative energy, negative people, and the path that society has laid for them, they would almost certainly find themselves moving towards prosperity. As the meeting went on, more and more of these residents began to confess to me their reasons for avoiding productivity.

Nearly all of them admitted that they had eluded personal change and settled with not improving their quality of living, because they never wanted to be considered "Booshie" (I'll talk more about the word "Booshie" later in the book) and possibly exiled by the members in their communities. Moreover, they felt that by advancing, they would no longer be able to relate to the project lifestyle. Although I enjoyed being within the presence of these brothers and sisters, I was initially blown away by this plead. As they continued to explain to me why they made a commitment to devalue their lives, as well as their children's lives to please their neighbors, I became mentally numb still trying to absorb their premises for living in poverty. Trying to remain calm, I covertly began to anger without showing any signs and immediately became a bit judgmental, even though I knew that was the wrong thing to do. Before I knew it, I found myself indicting all *blacks* living within low-income environments, these brothers and sisters in particular, of thinking with a slave mentality.

> *"Poverty is wrenching ... Tortuous ...*
> *Tormenting. It strips a person of the ability*
> *to give ... to bless ... to make a contribution*
> *to others. Don't tolerate it."*
> *-Anonymous*

For some reason, I could not help but to equate this self-defeated method of thinking to that of a slave. But after careful evaluation of a true slave's state of mind and making mental notes in my note pad, I quickly concluded that a slave's mentality was one of constant ingenuity, constant active rebellion against an oppressive society and environment, as well as constant struggle for equality and human rights, even if it meant risking their lives. Far from the attitude of *blacks* today, slave's interest consisted of everything that a vast number reject. Case in point, slaves wanted to help one another, longed to be married, desired some type of formal education, and risked their lives to get it, despite the fact that it was against the law. Too, unlike *blacks* today, slaves sought any window of opportunity that would lead to their freedom. Lack of education, or the effects of not having it, is the only parallel that does link low-income *blacks* of today to slaves.

Slaves who could not read and write proficiently were less likely to evaluate escape and were unable to cognitively function on their own. *Blacks* living in poverty today are stamped with this same dilemma. Those with very limited or no education are financially and socially immobile and cannot out run their modern-day plantations—the "hoods" they currently live within and rules and regulations which force them to be solely dependent upon "Daddy Government" to be taken care of. Were a slave to come pay a visit to America's ghettos right now, they'd be horrified to know that these are the distant offspring for whom they were beaten, raped repeatedly, mutilated, psychologically razed, and unwillingly sacrificed their families for. The development of these self-inflicted attitudes has crippled not only a massive number of *black* adults, but their children as well. A large number of *black* children, today, are performing at sub-par levels in school, because of the lack of all around support they are receiving at home. No one in the home is productive and their parent's biggest worry is deciding which club they will hit up on the weekend. In the mean time, their children are struggling gravely in school and being retained each school year, creating a cycle of failed living. Is this way of thinking, the cognitive counter-intelligence that *blacks* exercise, specifically those living within low-income areas across America, how society wants them to think? Is this whole idea of ghettos and housing projects a well structured and thought out sketch that has been put into effect to unendingly continue slavery into the future? I'm not personally excited about the use of the (N) word, especially labeling my people with it, but I sincerely believe that when someone *black* chooses to live in destitution when they are consciously aware of the fact that they do not have to and feel compelled to purposely set obstacles in the path of other *blacks* to satisfy their own selfish gratifications and appetites for envy, they are inviting room for that label to be issued to them. I will discuss the (N) word further in a later chapter.

Again, this may sound a bit harsh, but I become overwhelmingly consumed with anger when *blacks*, as an entire race, sell themselves short and then attempt to prevent other *blacks* from progressing, mainly, because they are devoted to promoting trivial acts via an unwillingness to modify their method of thinking while authorizing their potential to go to waste. I'm exceedingly angered when we (*blacks*) reject even the smallest window of opportunity that could possibly provide an outlet to a bigger break. Instead of seizing opportunities, we are continuously finding ways to exemplify unscrupulous behaviors that our counter-parts desire us to display. James Baldwin infamously exclaimed, ***"You can only be destroyed by believing that you really are what the white world calls a Nigger."*** Mr. Baldwin knew all too well that if *blacks* displayed the conduct of the (N) word, they may as well had been laboring for the oppressor; but more importantly, he was aware of the fact that *blacks* are far more talented than what the white world would ever admit. Just as Mr. Baldwin, I too know that we (*blacks*) are far from the six letter word that continues to haunt us and that our God given talents are superfluous. Even still, I am aware that when you are in battle, you never kill a man who is about to commit suicide. At this current moment, *blacks* in low-income environments are doing just that.

To all my *black* sisters and brothers in the struggle, reflect on this interesting paradox with humility. Whites, as well as associated races, strappingly desire to acquire and masquerade our qualities, deep down, minus the horrific eventualities that haunt us. This paradox may be too untamed for some to grasp a hold of, but contemplate this. If we were never distinguished as being powerful and influential, why would America's most revered possession, the white race, ravage their entire life existence trying to benumb us? Such a question does not inescapably compel one to produce an answer with the intentions of defending the premise; rather, the defensive angle here is the fact that we, as a complete race, have been wanted dead or alive since our initial existence in America. Still, we have managed to maintain our sanity and situate countless innovative principles for maneuvering while giving swagger and strength a new definition. Counter-parts, ranging from those who man cash registers to those who dwell within high profile bureaus, intensely desire our instinctive aura, grandeur, ability to endure, and assurance, while white youth living within trailer park developments, as well as suburban communities, listen to all of our R&B and rap music, mimic our gestures, nonsensical dress codes, strides, and vernacular—even our cunning use of "Ebonics".

While gathering data for *Ghetto Othello* at a bookstore I sporadically visit in Durham, N.C., I was met by the likes of five white teenage males who stormed into the section where I was sitting—all armed with leased swagger and distinctive ditty-bops which could have only been acquired from closely monitoring *black* culture. As they trotted through the aisles, each teen displayed an aggression, one relatively parallel to that which *blacks* naturally possess and exploit as an idiosyncratic defense mechanism on an *as need* basis, only amongst themselves though—fully aware of the fact that the cultural facade they simulated would only be respected and taken seriously within their emulated fraternity. Colored in the robust residue of hardcore gangsta rap music, which extended from an iphone one was carrying, their attitudes, dress code (oversized hooded shirts and saggin jeans), and diction, although each immensely struggled, verbally, trying to ride the tempo of the rapper's rhyme rhythm, all undeniably emulated *black* culture.

Further proof of this observation is easily unearthed every summer as they rush to tanning salons, beaches, lakes, and pool sides only to lie in the blistering sun and willingly endure excruciating pain from violent sun rays for hours while they listlessly risk their lives to skin cancer—just to become two shades darker. And if that's not enough attestation, white women desiring to possess a *black* woman's features run off and get doctored up, annually, spending thousands of dollars on chest, butt, and lip enhancing implants, while white men risk their lives by ingesting pills that are expected to provide them bodily and penis augmentations *black* men naturally possess.

Again, as much as they aspire to emulate us, they have no aspirations of actually being us. Here is another interesting paradox. As much as *blacks,* both men and women, are revered by white America for executing pivotal roles in various modes of entertainment they find therapeutic, the moment we remove ourselves away from microscopic view, appear in person, and probe metropolitan boulevards, chiefly when stars radiate the sky, within any city, all bets are off. My point here is not to transmit a negative and racist undertone, but to instead highlight what I find to be true, as well as provide concrete substantiation that, we, whether you want to believe or not, are highly sought to be emulated and are envied by numerous races, in particular our counter-parts—although we are aligned perfectly within the racial crosshair in America. Therefore, as a people who have had several odds stacked up against us from the first day we stepped foot into this country, we must cognitively warehouse this actuality, use this as fuel to power our attitudes, and strive for the success that is rightly ours.

QUIZ 1

- Is the self-defeated attitude that *blacks* continually exercise a learned behavior or is it embedded deep within as a stern result of the anguish of slavery? Explain in detail.

_____

_____

_____

_____

- Why do some brothers and sisters living in housing projects believe that way of living is normal and has been predestined for them to live, but don't realize that way of life should be viewed as a pit stop to independency? Explain in detail.

_____

_____

_____

_____

- Why does someone else's success breed envy and anger from those who are close to them? Explain in detail.

_____

_____

_____

_____

- **Do you feel that the actions of *blacks* who are struggling for position today replicate the actions of *blacks* who were slaves? As you answer this question, do not forget to highlight whether the actions are good or bad.**

_____

_____

_____

_____

- **Why do *blacks* exercise the "crab in the bucket syndrome" by pulling down someone who attempts to better themselves? Explain in detail.**

_____

_____

_____

_____

IDENTITY SEARCH, STEREOTYPES, PRISON

When speaking on the theme of identity, today, a great deal of *black* men and women are profoundly relying on brand names, money, immaterial items, and personal reputations to define their existence. Is this means of thinking somehow an allegiance to what they truly consider success to be or do they genuinely see themselves, above all, through a racial lens which mirrors the views of our oppressors? Therefore to temporarily escape their *reality*, a world that presses stern requirements upon them, requirements they find to be unattainable in order to be considered relevant, they exercise this method of thinking as an escape mechanism to flee into their own worlds—utopias free from oppression.

One phenomenon that has found a way to take on a life of its own and penetrate deep within the *black* race is the love of the bling bling, high dollar fashions, and the mental yielding to possessions that are insubstantial—mainly entities that will not prove to help us prosper or relinquish any value long-term. A core problem with this phenomenon is despite having an unpolluted exterior image of ourselves, feeling good about the high-dollar fashions which decorate us, what we are driving, and how much monetary leverage we possess, internally we are disgusted. Deep down we are paining from personal and emotional struggles. This is one of the primary reasons why most of our lives we are repetitively in search of an identity in which we deem credible in the eyes of society. Decade after decade, *blacks* have aggressively dieted on America's forged panaceas with the intentions of becoming fit, but the unceasing consumption of unwholesome sustenance has only resulted in our intrinsic ambitions becoming listless as we ignore personal change and what we need to do, individually, in order to improve the quality of our own lives. We continue to listen to white America report to us that pushing dope, sports, robbing one another for pennies, and meticulously searching for million dollar record deals are the only methods for *blacks* to make a judicious living— ignoring education. While there is nothing remotely wrong with desiring to become a professional athlete or recording artist, those are not the only avenues to success that are available for *blacks* to explore here in America.

One tear-jerking trend that has saturated young *black* aspiring athletes is what happens in their lives when they do not make the pros and their days of playing sports are over. A large majority of *black* male athletes, more specifically those who played high school sports at a sky-scraping level, are either struggling to get admitted or do not get accepted into college at all, due to academic insufficiency. And for an even slimmer number of *black* athletes who have managed to successfully penetrate college admission buildings and go on to play on the collegiate level, they are not graduating.

It's damaging enough that these young men are not finishing school, but what's even more tragic is that instead of returning to school to pursue some type of sports related profession, such as coaching, becoming a sports agent, or trainer, they all seem to be living out their alternative dreams as hustlers and drug dealers, transitioning from the court and athletic fields to the streets. The " I gotta have it right now mentality" has these young men, predominantly the brothers who were unable to meet any college's entry ideologies, glorifying the streets and life as a hustler in order to pursue the life that they believed professional sports would have provided them.

> *"More African American men are in prison*
> *or jail, on probation or parole than*
> *were enslaved in 1850,*
> *before the Civil War began,"*
> *-Michelle Alexander*

It has been demonstrated repeatedly within America that ordinary social identities and contingencies place *blacks* behind the eight ball: age, gender, finances, lack of education, strength of social circles, and more than ever, skin color. In reference to playing collegiate sports, white males who do not make the pros are embraced by America as they revert back to the professional world with a concrete atlas for their lives. Unaltered by the plights in which *black* males find impossible to elude, these individuals are able to maximize the use of their undergraduate degrees, and in a substantial number of cases, go on to pursue graduate degrees. The same contingencies that sting *black* men viciously champion and pose no threat to white men. This is chiefly, because white men mirror authentic social change according to America's principles. Not to mention, America protects her investments. The contingencies that haunt *blacks* today have been around for four hundred plus years—carrying out the same task. Even with that being highlighted, although being *black* today is an obscured entity for non-*blacks* to comprehend, I strongly feel that now is the best time, since the existence of our race in America, to be *black*. Albeit, two of the most vital mistakes that we (*blacks*) are continually making are ignoring and refusing to read the fine print of the unwritten *"Survival Guide for Blacks in America"* that history has chronicled and given to us, which states the following:

> **To increase your chances of surviving in America, you *must* be open to unlimited opportunities in which you never knew existed and it is very sound chance that these opportunities may exist outside of your personal environment, outside of your comfort zone. Also, no matter if you are male or female, you *must* not settle for level one success; paradigms of level one success are just finishing high school or obtaining a job that does not offer you the chance to advance vertically within the company. And most importantly, you *must* sever ties with the thinking inside of the box mentality, because this mentality will keep you in the same frame of mind day after day, year after year, and before you know it, ten years will pass you by and you will have the same job, same salary, same mentality, same friends, same attitude, and same lifestyle, wondering why you have**

not remotely budged spiritually, financially, professionally, or socially.

Surely, refusing to carefully analyze and mediate on this guide will not suffice in route to prosperity.

Furthermore, at some point you will have to reinvent yourself and shed off archaic methods of thinking, speaking, and functioning on a day to day basis. When you decide that you truly want to escape your outdated way of living, remaining the same person you were before transitioning to prosperity is not an option. Of all of the points involved in productive self-metamorphosis that must be met in order to transition to any tier of prosperity, reinventing yourself may be the most important single entity. Here is where you have to arrive at your future and recognize that failure is an event, not a person. An important aspect of reinventing yourself is pinpointing and utilizing all of the components of the niche that God has given you and diligently seeking a way to connect those components. These points are important primarily, because it takes a lot more than a content disposition in order for *blacks* to survive America's challenges. Keep this very critical reality in the forefront of your thoughts. Below is what I like to refer to as a redemption paradigm that will allow you to turn your life around.

RESTORATION PROCESS

- Desire to be free from bondage.
- Let go of the Past. That baggage is useless where you're headed.
- Renew your mind.
- Renounce outdated practices.

- Change your attitude and environment.
- Disconnect away from negative relationships: professional, friends and family, significant others.

Again, although the intimidations which haunted *blacks* generations earlier are not gone, they are unquestionably a lot more lenient and less intoxicating for *blacks* today to deal with. Still, for some reason, we (*blacks*) continue to run on destructive race tracks in pursuit of ghetto success— success that America does not acknowledge and has neither substance nor longevity. In the process of chasing conjured and non-tangible accomplishments, a vast majority of *black* men and women have wasted so much vital time that they have missed their children grow up, created a self-made prison for themselves, and failed to leave their personal worlds. In even more severe plights, due to extreme exhaustion from running in the fast lane to nowhere all of their lives, a number of *blacks* have run so hard for so long that their health has literally began to depreciate and they have physically lapsed at an early age.

I'm reminded of an incident that involved a young student who I was assigned to while working as a Reading Specialist. This particular student, although fragile in reading, was a very bright individual with strong aspirations of wanting to become a rapper and also had a fondness of designer fashions. I would always tell him, "There is nothing at all wrong with looking good, but that should not be your motivation in school or in life." Eventually, I had to explain to the young student the point I was making, which was he should not allow materialistic items, for instance, clothes, money, and shoes to be a top priority for him or else those entities would become his motivation in life. I also explained to the young gentleman that people, especially those who live in a self-created world of materialism, think on a very small scale.

So that this particular young student would be reading on grade-level by the end of the school year, I devised skill set prepping activities that catered to his deficiencies, but I needed his mother to assist me in helping him by reinforcing particular lessons *everyday* when he left school. To inform her of her child's ailment in the area of reading, as well as present to her exactly what I would need for her to do once he arrived home from school each day, I arranged a conference for the two of us to congregate. When she arrived to my office, I had no choice but to notice that the young lady was bathed in designer fashion from head to toe—Louis Vuitton hat, shoes, bag, and belt, which by the way, were not at all authentic. My immediate attention to what she was wearing did not compel me to conceive judgment against her, nor did I develop any personal off-putting feelings towards the young lady. Meeting her for the first time only put things in perspective for me in reference to what she valued, was possibly chasing, and the effort she put into chasing it. Surely, whatever she was chasing within her personal world was what shoved her to disregard the deficiency that her son was suffering from within the subject area of reading. Eventually, through this encounter, I discovered that ghetto success and everything the "hood" had to offer was the path that she was treading on.

In reference to her son, through careful examination of his student file, I discovered that he had the same dilemma a year prior to me arriving to that particular school, so surely she was aware of her son's deficiency in reading, right? I ask this question, because this type of deficiency was not something that he just all of a sudden developed over night. If this parent was ever aware of her son's deficiency, why didn't she reach out to school officials, in reference to helping him, long before I contacted her? Was his deficiency ignored at home, principally, because within her personal world education was not a top priority next to designer fashions, self-importance, props, and notoriety in the "hood"?

If you were to really zero in on *blacks'* actions and attitudes, especially those who have been inundated by the winds of "hood" policies, as a unit, it's almost as if they articulate, "We've never substantially had anything to call our own here in America; therefore, we are going to glorify "hood" policies and vehemently make everything that America considers wrong, work in our favor, because we are owed so much." A few illustrations that mirror this attitude include the unbroken and horrific use of the (N) word, provocative and disrespectful dress codes, the unremitting affixation to victimhood and underachievement, rebellion for authority, and the ideology that a *black* person who speaks proper English sounds white; therefore, (Ebonics) is the chosen language which represents an "authentic" *black*.

An immense number of *blacks* are unaware of the fact that being *black*, today, does not mean we must construct domiciles of ignorance and permanently reside within these quarters, but instead, to be *black* in America essentially means resisting white society's expectations of us, the temptations of the "hood", treacherous metropolitan avenues, and all of their deadly measures, even though, since day one in this country, that seems to be what we (*blacks*) have only been given to toil with. Every since we took our first step on this country's soil, America has tactically duped us into believing, immeasurably, in counter-productivity while it infinitely profited on the luxuries of interminable physical labor at the expense of *blacks*. The following are the receipts that bid proof: the structure of this country, the construction of the mansion at 1600 Pennsylvania Avenue, dehumanization of the oppressed, inventions that we (*blacks*) never received credit for, and land we were forced to submit. In return, we have only been given the repugnant assortments from those labor banquets and it's from those assortments that we (*blacks*) have been forced to subsist. An attention-grabbing paradox, though, is that although America has maintained first-rate health from consumption of vigorous *black* labor since infancy, as she matures in age, she is leisurely becoming queasy, weakened from her own tainted home grown products—corrupt greedy mongers: The George W. Bush administration, predatory lenders; Enron; Halliburton; Adelphia Communications; Savings and Loans (1980); and Bernie Madoff.

Even so, we must recognize that the promise that's co-ordinated by counter-productivity intensifies the urge for one to continue to practice failure, which in itself is very seductive, enticing, and has only deadly consequences. In fact, proof that validates counter-productivity's seductive-ness is found in the vast number of cases of *blacks* who have been fortunate enough to elude poverty's bear hug but are still, obliviously, finding themselves exiting their world of values and morals, jeopardizing everything they have worked so hard for, risking the leverage that their post-graduate educations, million dollar athletic talents, mega recording deals, elevated annual salaries, and self-created businesses have provided them only to revisit the "hood" and its policies via cognitive or tangible excursion for the sake of meshing with the people they knew before transitioning to prosperity. We've seen proof of this through the lives of NFL players Mike Vick, Sam Hurd, Adam Pacman Jones, Plaxico Burress, OJ Simpson, and rapper Beanie Sigal. Just as counter-productivity propagates failure through astute enchantment, the submission which extends away from America's "hoods" is radioactive and has a shrewd and silent method of luring one in, while at the same time vocalizing so deafening, especially to the brothers and sisters who are socially and morally bankrupt, desperately in need of love, and trying significantly to escape feelings of rejection. By and large, the streets are so appealing to *blacks*, because they somehow offer a place of profound belonging, extreme comfort, and for most, it is the only jurisdiction where they actually feel as if they are somebody.

I find it interesting that America's inner-city streets are policed and controlled by the hustlers and street soldiers, while the world seems to be controlled by our counter-parts. By controlled I mean, in the streets, what we (*blacks*) are striving to conquer does not nearly compare to what our counter-parts are striving to conquer. I'm heartbroken to report this, but for us (*blacks*) it seems as if cars, rims, shoes, titles attached to names, and street credibility is where we are currently peaking out, while our counter-parts are investing, owning shares, buying properties, and then renting those same properties back to us.

In terms of the racial bias that continues to prevent *blacks* from gaining any type of financial leverage in America today, uncontested, certainly there is probable cause to comprehensively cross-examine white America for exercising ethnic inequitableness, as well as their Machiavellian motives to strategically position us (*blacks*) in circumstances where we are still being forced to survive by any means necessary. So with that in mind, you should know that there is nothing wrong, in any way, with aspiring to seek understanding for their unmerited decision to camouflage injustice with fine print, which has affected *blacks* unswervingly, especially in the areas of education, race relations, equality, and social regulations. All are blatantly and ethically unbalanced. Even though, a major quandary in reference to this phenomenon is that we (*blacks*) have relinquished our right to diligently cross-examine, and instead, turned a blind eye, disregarded the rules that govern society, and chose to rebel and continue to display to America all of the routine inconsistencies we have amassed from metropolitan avenue civilization and the "hood".

For decades, we have hindered our own progress on this journey to prosperity by conforming to the stereotypes of the "hood". The "hood's" statutes as well as its expectations of us have both poisoned our minds gravely and ingeniously persuaded us to believe that there is such a thing as an "authentic" *black* person. As well, the "hood" has manufactured and made passable all of the characteristics of how these man-made *blacks* should act, talk, walk, think, and conduct themselves. Every since it was created by America for the purpose of excluding *blacks* from existing within society alongside our white counter-parts, the "hood" has gradually transitioned from a garrison where *blacks* once meshed in order to survive to a setting that now conditions us to disregard the important aspects of what is needed to attempt to augment *black* life, such as a sound education and various resources that could possibly introduce us to a world of prosperity.

In every "hood" across the country, street policies have duped *blacks* into believing that such a destructive mode of thinking is ok. Although conforming to regulations of the "hood" may seem pleasing, in reality, this poisonous method of ruminating is part of the reason why a great deal of *black* men and women are in the state that they are in today and have never fully married their true identity. I am highly aware of the fact that everyone, at some point in their life, searches for an identity that provides them current comfort, but it's vital that we (*blacks*) shed off the expectations of "hood" life and its "keeping it real mentality", because that mentality contradicts the life that will assist us in reaching prosperity at any level.

The hardest working man in show business, entertainer James Brown, and the best boxer of all time, Mohammad Ali, are two African American heroes whose legacies are vital to *black* history. They both, through their respected art forms, music and professional boxing, rejected what the white world attempted to inflict upon them. I make mention of these two icons, because they forced the white world during the sixties, (a time when racism was at its apex), to come to terms with the fact that *blacks* were a lot more skilled and talented than they had credited. James Brown went against the grain when he delivered his hit song in 1968, *Say it Loud, I'm Black and I'm Proud*. This song in particular, in addition to an agglomeration of others that Mr. Brown wrote such as *Mind Power*, addressed racial prejudice against *blacks* as well as the need for them to become mentally and financially liberated, so that they would no longer be conformed to the grasp of the white oppressors methods of operations. In this song, Mr. Brown proclaimed, *"We done made us a chance to do for ourself/we're tired of beating our head against the wall/workin' for someone else".* This was just one of the many lines that profoundly made its mark on the subject of race relations and allowed *blacks* a chance to be heard. To the masses, this particular song was an anthem that stated, "I'm *black*, proud, and I have just as much ability as any white man," and they stood on this belief. Mr. Brown, within his long list of hit songs, captivated his listeners with his groovy way of orally orchestrating, piercing horns, funky lead guitars, and multiple drummers, while at the same time making *blacks* dance and forget about all of their troubles.

Mohammad Ali, as well, exemplified his love for not only being a *black* man but also love for the *black* race through his charismatic demeanor as a heavy weight boxer and the way he flirted with words to formulate rhymes that predicted how he would knock out his upcoming opponent. But his most epic stand happened not within the ring, but when Mr. Ali looked white America dead in the face and confronted each of its oppressive ideologies by refusing the draft and not entering the army, in addition to refusing to apologize for the unpatriotic remarks he made in reference to the Vietnam War. Even though he would eventually be tried, convicted, sentenced to five years in prison, stripped of his boxing license, and ordered to pay a *$10,000* fine, his stand against racial inequality was stout and inspired all, even whites. Ali's draft refusal is monumental in the *black* community today and was a performance that single-handedly elevated him to a plateau in which he was knighted by all *blacks* into *Black* manhood, *Black* courage, and *Black* pride.

I personally believe that although Mr. Ali was extremely talented and his skill as a heavy weight was unmatchable during his prime, the state that the *black* race was in during the sixties was his stimulus to train hard and beat his opponents viciously. Not only was Mr. Ali fighting against an opponent on the other side of the ring waiting to inflict deadly force upon him, he was also fighting against the white world and their oppressive mentalities and agendas.

James Brown and Muhammad Ali were both truly devoted to their spirituality as well, which was the catalyst that drove them to be the voice for all *blacks* who were struggling to embrace social equality, as they publicly spoke without fearing for their lives—saying things the average *black* civilian would have been killed for.

In order to be able to reject what the white world expects of us, at some point, we all must develop a stout relationship with God and allow that vertical connection to give us an unyielding understanding of our true merit and value, so that we do not have to seek confirmation of belonging from materialistic items or even other people. An established fact is that we all, even the so called toughest individuals, need to feel wanted by others, but what seldom goes unnoticed is the fact that we must seek this comfort first and foremost from the most credible source of all. So then, it is vital we commit to memory that we are all children of God, created in his image, endowed with his assistance, and set free by his grace. Being cognitively aware of these decrees is good, but above all, believing them to be true in your heart is the tool which will allow you to detach yourself away from intangible and harmful identities. Cleary understand that I am not using this tome as a vessel to argue about who's going to church and who's not. I am only implying that I unsympathetically believe a coherent relationship with God teaches the necessity of self-worth and submission that one needs in order to truly see themselves as valuable.

Black men and women, young and old, are still struggling to find themselves as well as their position within society simply, because they have not genuinely unshackled personal obstructions and mishaps from their past, they fear the path to success as well as what that path will require of them, and are content with where they currently exist in life. All of these concerns have seized and imprisoned *blacks* in their search for what they consider to be an agreeable ideology that is married to the term 'keeping it real', which is "authentic" *blackness*. It almost seems as if *blacks* are afraid they will have their ghetto cards revoked if they do not perpetually 'keep it real' and relinquish their right to abort their search for "authentic" *blackness*.

I found Zadie Smith's article, *Speaking in Tongues*, which surfaced in the February, 2009 issue of the *New York Review of Books,* and what she enveloped on the meaning of the term 'keeping it real' to be very attention-grabbing. Smith covered a vast amount of ground as she discussed the authentic premise for this term, which was initially intended to create a unified *black* voice in order to fortify the *black* race. Smith's ideology of the term's meaning, today, corresponds with what I believe, which is, it has been ruthlessly warped. Smith wrote, "Today, we have confined and restricted it. To me, the instruction 'keep it real' is a sort of prison cell, two feet by five. The fact is, it's too narrow. I just can't live comfortably in there." Smith continued, "It made *blackness* a quality each individual *black* person was constantly in danger of losing. And almost anything could trigger the loss of one's *blackness*: attending certain universities, an impressive variety of jobs, a fondness for opera, a white girlfriend, an interest in golf, and of course, any change in voice."

Who do we really want to be, ourselves, students, gangstas, scholars, high maintenance video chics, thug rappers, or the big time narcotics tycoon everyone knows in the "hood"? The move from *Poverty to Prosperity* will never be made if we continue to make ourselves prisoners of our own desirable search for "authentic" *blackness*.

I recently over heard one of my colleagues ranting in regards to the decisions she would make if she just happened to win the lottery's mega millions. Her proposal was one of short-term financial execution that would assure her to be utterly broke within a year after winning. My colleague's plan consisted of unvarying spending and no planning or wealth building for the future. As she prolonged, I soon realized, according to her financial decision making, that my colleague, although a very bright woman, was still in search of her identity. She endlessly deliberated on the topic of countless materialistic items and personal transformations she deemed necessary to have that would bring her instant gratification. Due to a never ending search for an identity, it seems that a vast number of *blacks*, more specifically when it comes to budgeting money, fail to see the validity in devising a tangible financial plan that will lead to building wealth long-term. All we know is spend, spend, spend, and spend, even when we do not have it. It's almost as if we are paying a fee to lease a position within society.

From day one in this new world, *blacks* were compelled to adapt to the visions and abhor proposals of white oppressors, but through adaptation our ancestors gained superior knowledge regarding survival. An interesting paradox that escapes me is that everything that our ancestors sought in order to obtain a better life as slaves, *blacks* today seem to disregard: a sound education, willingness to assist one another, structuring the two-parent home, and a substantial plan to build wealth. They may not have known much about the logistics of keeping books and accounting, but they certainly knew how to save and were aware of the fact that owning your own land was an assured avenue to building wealth. More importantly, these great men and women were not blind to the fact that an education was one of the most essential tools they could have obtained during their tenure as slaves. Aware of the importance of a sound education, some risked their lives as they sought even the most minute window of opportunity that would possibly allow them to learn to read, write, and calculate within a world of demonic tyranny by clandestinely and unlawfully trying to educate themselves, fully aware of the fact that for them education was off limits and carried a penalty of death if ever caught trying to pursue it. Reflect on the following actual affidavits of enslaved *blacks* when asked about wanting to become educated.

George Thompson, enslaved in Kentucky, and the following slaves were interviewed in 1937 by the *Federal Writers' Project of the Works Progress Administration*, and in this interview, Mr. Thompson was quoted saying, "Our master would not allow us to have any books and when we were lucky enough to own a book we would have to keep it hid, for if our master would find us with a book he would whip us and take the book from us." Thompson continued, "After receiving three severe whippings, I gave up and never again tried for any learning and to this day I can neither read nor write."

John W. Fields gave his testimony as a slave deterred from education when he stated, "In most of us colored folks was the greatest desire to be able to read and write. We took advantage of every opportunity to educate ourselves. The greater part of the plantation owners were very harsh if we were caught trying to learn or write." Fields resumed, "It was the law that if a white man was caught trying to educate a negro slave, he was liable to prosecution. Our ignorance was the greatest hold the South had on us."

Susan Snow, enslaved in Alabama, when asked about becoming educated stated, "Us didn' have no schoolin. Us could go to school wid de white chillun if us wanted to, but didn' nobody teach us. I's educated, but I aint educated in de books. I's educated by de licks an' bumps I got."

Lorenza Ezell, enslaved in South Carolina, was interviewed in Texas. She replied, "I ain't never been to school but I jes' pick up readin'. With some my first money I ever earn I buy me a old blue-back Webster. I carry dat book wherever I goes. When I plows down a row, I stop at de end to rest and den I overlook de lesson. I' member one de very first lessons was "Evil communications 'rupts good morals". I been done use dat lesson all my life."

Hal Hutson, enslaved in Tennessee, was interviewed in Oklahoma, Ca. in 1937. Mr. Hutson, one of the few slaves who could actually read, write, and calculate, testified, "I learned to read, write, and figger [figure: do Math] at an early age. Master Brown's boy and I were the same age you see (14 years old) and he would send me to school to protect his kids, and I would have to sit up there until school was out. So while sitting there I listened to what the white teacher was telling the kids, and caught on how to read, write, and figger—but I never let on, 'cause if I was caught trying to read or figger dey would whip me something terrible." Hutson concluded, "After I caught on how to figger the white kids would ask me to teach them."

Today, the gap between *blacks* who are educated and have managed to make it into a class that is somewhat privileged and those who have not has grown increasingly wide. This is a direct result of middle class values and principles not being embraced within *black* low-income localities; instead, these values and principles are scorned and unassociated with "authentic" *blackness*. I want my brothers and sisters who have not yet tapped into the power they possess, which will surely guide them to prosperity, to understand something. The entire *black* race has been genetically tainted with the blood of every slave who has escaped to freedom as well as those who lost their lives trying; therefore, we have within us the ability to break free of every iron grip that has been placed upon us, including self-doubt. Devine A. Robinson, author of *Blacks: From the Plantation to the Prison*, concurred with this same ideology and vindicated this very premise when he wrote:

> I view *Black* Americans to be descendants of strength. This is because if you made it through the Middle Passage, you were of strong qualities. These qualities would soon rise to the occasion and go against the grain of the institute of slavery but not without first being crucially conditioned and not without meeting tremendous opposition.

Whether it is a deficiency in learning math, problems with some particular addiction, or low self-esteem, we can overcome them all. Even still, there are an excessive number of *blacks* who cannot wrap their minds around the fact that they actually possess the apparatus to defeat their past. My personal assessment of this ill-bred method of thinking is that it stems from white America's continual reinforcement of *black* stereotypes as well as the masses being tackled and subdued by society's expectations of their own cognitive ability.

THE DANGERS OF STEREOTYPES

From an early age, through movies, music, the "hood", and society's windows, *blacks* are conditioned to believe that there just may be a well-built possibility that we are not good enough for America. So, as a youngster growing up with no tangible and physical positive examples to pattern ourselves after, what happens when we merge our own idea of "authentic" *blackness* with what society feeds us? Exactly, as a result of consuming unhealthy wisdom, our ability to see beyond our personal worlds slowly deteriorates and soon diminishes. We begin to doubt anything that is related to success, especially success that involves utilizing cognitive ability. We also develop and carry within us a disadvantaged spirit. This is why it is imperative we break away from stereotypes. Mentioning that, let's explore the power of stereotypes, or what I call "the threat". There was a time when *blacks* were mimicked by caricatures—white actors with their faces painted dark *black* whose intentions where to distort the essence of all *blacks*. The primary premise behind this vicious act was to psychologically inject whites with negative stereotypical ideologies about *blacks* which suggested that we were nothing but big lip, big nose, beast like, and lazy good for nothing animals who were only allowed to occupy a place in society to be a white man's slave. Even though the images that those white actors painted for the white world to believe about *black* people were counter-intuitive, the threat of being executed for not living up to what was expected of them forced *blacks* during that time to intentionally live out negative stereotypes. An issue that I have with *blacks* today is that we, unlike our ancestors, choose to live out negative stereotypes even though we are not compelled, even though we no longer have to worry about the threat of being executed if we choose not to. Here is where we are condemning ourselves rapidly.

In reference to African Americans, the word stereotype is "the threat" that we continue to allow land us in prison, keep our children from performing at grade level in school, and dupe us into believing that prosperity beyond the 'hood" doesn't exists, at least for *blacks* to obtain. Every negative stereotype of *blacks* that society, movies, and the media highlights seems to be exactly what *blacks* firmly relate to, primarily *black* men. Basically, we are doing exactly what the white world desires us to do by leading all nationalities in every negative statistic, continuing to take each other's lives, and most devastating of all, hating ourselves. These actions constitute that we have not yet secured an undeviating identity collectively.

Is it secure to insinuate that a large number of *black* men feel inferior to white men in this unbalanced society we live in, because surely their actions do not convey that they have confidence in themselves? And if so, do these low-grade feelings they conceal and bear stem from childhood events or is this an affliction that has been genetically embedded deep within their DNA as a result of slavery? In *Incidents in the Life of a Slave Girl*, published in 2001, Harriet Jacobs weighed in on the state of the *black* man during her tenure as a slave and how white slave masters had driven him to feel less than a man. I found her assessment thought-provoking, mainly, because Jacob's description of the *black* man then, mirrors precisely that of the *black* man today. Ms. Jacobs exclaimed, "I admit that the *black* man is inferior. But what is it that makes him so?" She continued, "It is the ignorance in which white men compel him to live; it is the torturing whip that lashes manhood out of him."

71

You must agree that the picture Ms. Jacobs painted makes a direct connection to the state of *black* men today. The unbalanced relationship between white and *black* men on her plantation in many ways mirrors the relationship that *black* men have with white men today. So then, is it safe to assume that the negative stereotypes that *black* men intentionally continue to act out, today, parallel the same ignorance in which the white world forced *blacks* on plantations to live out during slavery and the self-doubt that is produced from that ignorance is the torturing whip that is lashing the manhood out of them?

Black men have falling victim to the vicious cycle of stereotypes. On the streets and in the "hood" is where the stereotypes, (the threats), are grooming *black* men to become modern day slaves. Once the seductive urge to transition into something or someone they deem as powerful has been met for the sake of seizing street credibility, the consequences from that metamorphosis then makes the transition from the streets to the modern day plantation, which is (prison), a reality. As a matter a fact, for those who are unaware, the modern day prison system mirrors the exact same plantations that bound our ancestors as slaves: one overseer, daily movement is dictated, perpetrators are considered property, rebuffed wages, and no escape attempts allowed.

A large number of *black* communities are suffering gravely, because the vast majority of *black* men within them have relinquished their rights to avoid stereotypes that our ancestors could not steer clear of, no matter how hard they tried. As a result, jail buses are leaning over, filled with *black* men, only because they feel that they have to live out the ignorance that society has disguised as a quasi self-fulfilling prophecy. In pursuing these illusions *black* men and women are moving backwards at high-speeds instead of moving forward and reaching for excellence.

ALARMING STATISTICS

At this very moment, we are observing a prevailing number of *black* men, in record figures, be incarcerated. According to prison statistical research performed by William J. Sabol, Ph.D, former Associate Director of Center on Urban Poverty and Social Change and Heather Conture, 15% of all *black* American men in their late teens to early thirties are currently on some type of disciplinary confinement or are behind bars, and a 2005 prison statistic revealed that *black* males in prison were jointly serving a 15,000,000 year prison term. This same prison statistic revealed that as of July 2006, there were almost 800,000 *black* males incarcerated in U.S. prisons and jails. Furthermore, at midyear 2007, *black* women were incarcerated at a rate six times that of white women (or 400 per 100,000 U.S. residents versus 70 per 100,000 U.S. residents). In addition, data from the Department of Justice revealed that a *black* male born today has a 29% chance of spending time in a state or federal prison during his lifetime. These numbers are alarming enough to make anyone question how we arrived at this particular point in our existence as a race, as well as make

Photos: AP/Wide World Photos

even the stoutest non-believers, all who have written off the possibility that there is a subliminal conspiracy to destroy the *black* race, reconsider. And if there is the possibility of a plot on the table, is there a remote chance that this conspiracy was purposely channeled through laws, school systems, academic administrations, politicians, and judges to penetrate to the core of the *black* race expeditiously, especially with the powers that be aware of the fact that an elevating high school dropout rate would unquestionably increase the arrest rate? These grave statistics mirror just what God tells us in Revelations 12 1:5, (*New International Version, 2011*).

> *[1] A great sign appeared in heaven: a woman clothed with the sun, with the moon under her feet and a crown of twelve stars on her head. 2 She was pregnant and cried out in pain as she was about to give birth. 3 Then another sign appeared in heaven: an enormous red dragon with seven heads and ten horns and seven crowns on its heads. 4 Its tail swept a third of the stars out of the sky and flung them to the earth. The dragon stood in front of the woman who was about to give birth, so that it might devour her child the moment he was born. 5 She gave birth to a son, a male child, who will rule all the nations with an iron scepter.*

As I stated earlier, even if you are not one to lean on conspiracy theories for support, you must ask yourself vital questions after coming in contact with these statistics. Are we living in a society that has set up tactics to purposely have these numbers the way they are? Is this system that we are up against setting up the most vulnerable people within low-income populations while pretending to assist them? Have laws from the beginning of time, more so the sixties and especially the eighties, been modified to target *blacks* and all minority groups with the intentions of asphyxiating them, while the middle and upper-class, primarily whites, continue to receive lighter sentences, second, third, fourth, and fifth chances in life, despite the offenses and crimes they commit? Even with a possible plot to destroy *blacks* on the table, I still find it unreal that *blacks* continue to fall into all of the purposely set traps, which as a result, are volleying our race back in forth between state and federal prison systems and the grave.

For those aware of the horrifying statistics that continue to demolish the *black* community, the numbers are anything but surprising. As for *black* men and women without an education and sound direction in America, street seduction is very tempting, especially if their homes had no type of family structure. Metropolitan avenues offer them a place of belonging or at least make them believe that. This brings me to my next point. What's the deal with this hazardous ego that *black* men are clasping to in the streets? This is an ego that mimics a toughness that can only be obtained by doing remorseless jail time in some of America's most unforgiving penitentiaries. It's escorted by crafty vernacular, a facial expression that screams antagonism, saggin pants (I will address this issue in the next chapter), and rigid verbal intercourse that cites ownership of scores of firearms, boasting of drug use, and possession of multiple women. It's as if gangsta qualities, firearms, and street smarts are now the new representation of a *black* man's genitals. Every time their toughness is tested, they seem to become egotiscally erect. What's dangerously poisonous about this particular attitude is that it coerces *black* men to propagate elapsed actions which are not germane to existing circumstances. This same egotistic boldness was utilized during slavery by a great deal of our ancestors, but during that time their lives depended on it. *Blacks* had no choice but to re-adjust and use their egos as sentinel devices due to the plights they were facing. Dr. Richard Williams, in his book *They Stole it But You Must Return It*, highlighted this very truth in reference to *black* slaves when he wrote, "When *Blacks* could not successfully use the first levels of coping mechanisms for survival and human dignity, many turned to the second level. The second level includes the ego-defense mechanisms. These mechanisms are used to protect the person's self-concept."

The ego in which *blacks*, chiefly *black* men, are obtaining from the streets is driving them to completely damage their futures and ignore their duties as parents. I find it captivating that *black* men and women today are actually proud of having been in detention centers and prison systems. I recently overheard two female students, between classes, glorifying and comparing their time spent in jail. If I'm not mistaking, isn't imprisonment a form of slavery and bondage? When did slavery become an achievement worth glorifying? What's even more dangerous is that *blacks* are passing these traits and rebellious methods of thinking down to their children and at the same time neglecting them as they grow up, which continues the cycle of destruction within the *black* race.

QUIZ 2

- If *blacks*, in particular *black* men, don't belong
  in detention centers, jails, and prisons, why can't
  they stay out of them? Contemplate this question
  conscientiously before answering, and then list
  all of the possible reasons that you can think of.

  _____

  _____

  _____

  _____

- Why do *black* men feel rejected by society and
  accepted by the prison system? Explain in detail.

  _____

  _____

  _____

  _____

- How can rehabilitation be effective if upon
  release felons cannot find work and there are
  no programs to help them transition back into
  society? Is this a calculated method of placing
  black men back in prison? Explain in detail.

  _____

  _____

  _____

  _____

- Does society truly expect *black* men and women
  to fail and have they accepted failure for themselves? Explain in detail.

  _____

_____

_____

_____

- **Have *blacks*, men and women, accepted exclusion from the life of our hosted country?**

_____

_____

_____

_____

sAGGIN SPELLED BACKWARDS, SOCIETY'S VIEW

I made the statement earlier, "I love my culture and race dearly, and will defend them both extensively, but I also do not have a problem, at all, condemning either of them when they are wrong for the sake of motivating them." Witnessing *black* men participate in the mortifying act of saggin their  pants immediately moves me to formulate and relinquish feelings of repugnance. These feelings are not utterly aimed towards these brothers with the intentions of me, personally, detesting them as individuals, but more so towards the mental poltergeist, the unseen specter which distinctively transports all of the cognitive residue from the "hood" directly to the frail sections of one's brain, for convincingly bathing their mentality and perception of what being a real *black* man is while simultaneously placing a finger over the peephole from which they view the world. Even though, these men still, considerably, possess authorization within this malevolent pact and the ability to recognize imprudence, which is why I am compelled to openly condemn and call out all who are condemning themselves to the subject of disgust by publicly exposing their underwear. Of all of the paralytic actions *black* men continue to exercise, via physical and cognitive implementation—this is one of the most potent and one that I personally despise. Let's just eject the race card away from the entire equation and approach this epidemic with the intentions of being truthful about it. No matter who saggs their pants, whites, *blacks*, Asians, males or females, the entire presentation just says, "Impertinent." One wearing their pants in such a fashion to purposely expose their under garments is very disrespectful and the primary reason I find this impediment so disturbing. I am entirely aware of the fact that all generations send social signals and saggin pants do not determine one's ability, but saggin your pants down beneath your butt is irrefutably the wrong signal to be sending the same society you will one day be summoned to and have to ask for a job.

In a recent column regarding an ordinance being implemented in Ft. Pierce, Florida that would possibly sanction the city to fine anyone for wearing saggin pants that revealed their underwear written by Anthony Westbury entitled *Saggy Pants Symbolize What's Gone Wrong in Black Community, Kids Say*, he admitted that he was initially against the ordinance. Mr. Westbury stated, "When I first heard about the call by Fort Pierce City Commissioner Reggie Sessions for a city ordinance banning saggy pants, I thought the District 1 representative had gotten his own pants wrapped too tightly around his head." It wasn't until

Anthony Westbury visited an after school program by the name of *Community Outreach Youth Program* that made him re-evaluate his feelings towards banning sagging pants. After sitting down and talking to young people between the ages of 15 and 21 about the saggin pants ordinance and asking them how they felt about it, he was shocked to hear that they were all for it. They felt that the act of someone saggin their pants was highly disrespectful and sympathized with older individuals who had to visually endure this hideous presentation. The young individuals who Mr. Westbury sat down with are all proof that being in the presence of positive energy and influence can change the mindset of anyone. In response to Mr. Westbury's column, someone anonymously wrote a rejoinder that read, *"I love this pants fad! It tells me who not to hire, or associate with."*

In relation to inappropriateness, this fashion statement that mainly *black* men are welcoming is equivalent to a female employee dressing unsuitable for the work place by wearing tight clothing too revealing to be worn in public. Saggin pants give ambiances of repulsiveness to those who witness the act, especially when out in public places such as the movies, restaurants, grocery stores, or mall. Who desires to see someone else's underwear when they are out with their family and children?

What truly makes this dress code even more disturbing is the insubordinate mentality that compliments it. Routinely, the brothers who wear their pants saggin down to their bottoms seem to all display the same attitude of rebellion and chauvinism as if the world should be enthralled by their large dose of vulgar fashion foolishness. This dress code is clearly sending the wrong message and was never meant to be fashionable. I wonder how many of the *black* males participating in this fashion statement, especially the so-called hardcore street soldiers, are aware of the rationale behind the saggin pants theory.

There are numerous truths in regards to the history of this fad and it being conceived on prison yards. The most popular truth is that saggin pants once highlighted who was available to be another man's companion on prison yards. That's right, for those who are unaware where the act of men saggin their pants was originated, its roots stem from prisoners who wore their pants low, because the absence of a belt was a customary way to introduce other men to homosexuality. Meanwhile, on the streets, the sagg exhibited signs of having been in prison; in turn, this became a trend that displayed toughness. In some localities, the lower the sagg, the harder one was perceived to be. Today, this fashion concept, which was derived in prison, has gained support from all cultures, primarily with *black* males, because it was able to make its way into the world of Rap culture. Given that it was symbolic of street life, the rap world immediately embraced saggin pants, ignoring the fact that it was connected to the ideology of homosexuality behind prison walls.

One of the many inaugurations one must succumb to in order to be accepted into the gangsta rap culture, one that is aimed above all at *black* men, is the fact that they must either appear to have been or have actually been to prison and accumulated a propagated criminal history which emphasizes their street credibility. Saggin pants have somehow become the chosen attire which links *black* men to gangs and thug life and are worn as a badge of delinquency. In some cases, the wearing of saggin pants is accompanied along with a distinctive walk that conveys thuggish swagger and disrespect for authority. I, as well as many others, just cannot wrap my mind around the reasoning behind a fashion statement which compels one to sagg their pants and then shortly after, persistently pull them up every five seconds. Again, what's the premise of saggin? For me, it is gravely sad to see *black* adult men in their 20's and 30's saggin their pants and continuously pulling them up, only for them to just fall down again.

To try to gain some type of reasoning for this act, I went to a credible source. In 2010, I spoke with one of my former students by the name of Demarcus Griggs, who on multiple occasions heard me say to him, "Pull your pants up before entering my classroom." Although this particular student submerged himself into a world that boasted of heavy duty gangsta rap culture, he was not at all isolated from reality; this young man was actually quite shrewd and well aware of all of the negative stigmas attached to this dress code. Demarcus, just as many other young *black* men who reside within America's metropolitan districts, is simply a product of his environment. While speaking with him, I found out that a great deal of *black* men, chiefly *black* men between the ages of 18 and 25 who he knew, sagged their pants low, because they felt rejected in some form or fashion by society. The individuals who he particularly made reference to were all young *black* men who either lived within the same environment in which he lived or were products of more rigorous ghettos. His chief intention for promoting this phenomenon not only stemmed from self-governing observation of his male peers and family members within his personal environment, men he came in contact with on a daily basis, but above all, from society's decision to completely write him off. This verbal exchange ultimately lead me to believe that *black* men, predominantly *black* males in their late teens to mid twenties, also use this dress code as one of many coping mechanisms to deal with America's rejection and to simply state to society, "You cannot tell us what to do or how to dress, especially if you are not helping us." After listening attentively to Demarcus's oration, I responded to his assessment by telling him that even though I did not agree with the dress code, I did indeed understand the premise for *black* men using the phenomenon as a means of coping with rejection, because rejection is painful, especially when it comes from those you trust. And at some point in all of our lives, even if we will not overtly admit it, *black* men have put a great deal of trust in America. Even though, exposing your underwear in public is absolutely the wrong ideology to embrace to express revolt. The last point that I made while speaking with Demarcus in reference to America's saggin pants scourge caused him to mentally subside. I made it comprehensible that the word "saggin" spelled backwards revealed the word in which society considers every *black* male who participates in this act.

What I find to be almost as sad as the concept itself is the fact that this discourteous dress policy is really important to *black* men. If something as invaluable as this improvident dress code is what *black* men are finding refuge in, what does this say about the future of *black* men? When will they begin to find value in entities that are far more tangible than revealing their undergarments? Again, it is not solely the act of these brothers saggin their pants that's keeping them from initiating an astute and well thought out plan of action needed in order for them to be able to at least, somewhat, counter the discriminatory gusts which awaits them as they trek on their purposely debris filled and elongated paths America has made available, exclusively, for them to travel in route to discovering prosperity, but more so the mental-ity they marry with it. In making that point, do not take my stance as exercising my right to be judgmental of brothers who sagg their pants. That ideology is not a reflection of my attitude, at all, in reference to this illogical act. All I'm affirming is what you brothers need to know, which is, what you respect is what you will attract. If you revere brothers who are in the streets saggin their pants beneath their butts then you are going to attract a particular mentality and the mentality affixed to that act surely counters any form of energy that will able you to transition to prosperity.

THE NEGATIVE EFFECTS OF SAGGIN PANTS

- You develop a mentality that obstructs your future
- This mentality clouds where you need to be; therefore, you never leave where you are
- Emulating a convict mentality can lead to convict consequences
- You become trapped in a negative mindset
- You send a message of rebellion to society
- You begin to view all avenues that lead to prosperity outside of the "hood" as weak
- You deter quality women from finding interest in you
- You automatically remove yourselves away from any job related opportunities

WHITES DARE TO ENTER

The fact that whites are partaking in this rebellious movement is proof that they are indeed followers of *black* fashion, swagger, and style-even if following puts them at risk of losing favor with America. What's unmistakably vivid is the fact that most, if not all, of the white males who sagg their pants have no earthly idea why they are doing it, aside from desperately attempting to toe the line of or be considered someone who can genuinely relate to and understand *black* culture. But what exactly do *blacks* possess that would make whites—uniquely white males—willingly tread on bayou soil laden with mines of bigotry, resentment, racial tension, profiling, and negative media stereotyping just to get a peek at what's going on inside of our world? What type of rousing credibility does someone white gain from risking it all by attempting to make their white correspondents believe that they are able to directly relate to *black* culture? A solid motive that comes to mind is one that is carved by their unyielding curiosity of African Americans—which is, they desperately desire to explore and obtain what they perceive to be "authentic" *blackness*. This phenomenon is quite interesting, because history has proven that they are already quite proverbial with a segment of *black* culture, one in which they created, that comes in the form of the boogie man—the (N) word.

Whites are fully aware of the fact that there is only one way to truly get a glance at the authenticity of *black* culture and that is by physically entering into the world of *blacks.* They have arrived at a point where they clearly understand, in terms of being familiar with our self-manufactured traditions, that boxing from the outside is no longer effective and offers them no chance of winning favor amongst their equals. They must, now, enter a ring that does not favor them any advantages and subject themselves to an itinerary of deadly strikes, all within the center of the squared circle. This speaks volumes, because we (*blacks*) already reside within a world that doesn't root for us, a world that really doesn't welcome us as blissfully as it should. Our world is interspersed with demons who wear masks as well as their deadly expectations which are powered by the boundless limits of their imagination. Again, it speaks volumes that whites and supplementary races are daring to enter into the world of *blacks* in search of a new personality, new swagger, and new nonchalance, because these are all of the things that we are typecasted and condemned for.

Mentioning this, here are two interesting paradoxes. The same world whites desire to enter is the same world *blacks* desire to leave and the same things they admire about *blacks* are the same things we are hated for. As I mentioned earlier, this proves that our race has a paramount relevance—one that is desired to be explored at all cost. What's also worthy of noting is the fact that our history even attracts foreign cultures. The verity that whites would even dare to enter into the world of *blacks* tells me that there is something exceptional that we have that they feel could enhance their social and personal repertoire.

Still, I urge *black* men to understand one important fact. If you're going to dress like a product of the streets, be prepared to be treated like a product of the streets. As well, if you want to advertise that you've tasted and consumed large doses of the victuals of prison life then get ready to be obstructed by law enforcement on various occasions and treated as if you have. Discern that you won't be obstructed, exclusively, because you're *black*; more than likely, it will be because of your dress code too. If you take an extremely good look at the populace committing crimes within your locality, such as street drug sales, home invasions, murders, and robberies, you will find that they all closely resemble one another, primarily, because they are all clothed the same. What type of message are you really sending? Nevertheless, I find it heartbreaking that *black* men continually insist on wanting to be affiliated with prison. Again, what's good about going to prison?

QUIZ 3

- Why is the term "acting white" paralleled with winning, but the term "acting *black*" contains multiple negative aspects and is affiliated with losing? Explain in detail.

_____

_____

_____

_____

- Why is it dangerous to affiliate with people who have peaked out, in reference to progressing in life, and can only affiliate with losing?

_____

_____

_____

_____

- In reference to saggin pants, is it possible that imitating the trend's origin will lead to one developing a prison mentality?

_____

_____

_____

_____

- If we are critical of *black* men saggin their pants, should we be just as critical of *black* women purposely exposing their undergarments when wearing low-rise jeans?

_____

_____

_____

_____

- **Do you feel that laws being passed around the country to band saggin pants are just modern day methods to continue exercising racism or merely a practice to attempt to clean up society?**

_____

_____

_____

_____

4

FÊTE

As a product of a single-family home and growing up in the inner-city, I never knew or understood the stipulations that needed to be met in order for one to be classified as low-income and poor, nor the qualifications that permitted a family to be able to live in the projects. Honestly, I just thought that people chose to live in the projects and they could just move in whenever there was a unit available, the same way that people living in the expensive apartments on the other side of the city did. I was also totally unaware that one's annual income dictated where they could or could not live and the less education you had, the more likely you would be living in the ghetto.

My mother, Ms. Rosetta Jones, is the true definition of a combatant—a woman who sacrificed her own livelihood and in numerous cases, her own happiness, for the sake of her children. I must also mention that she is the most optimistic person that I have ever met. Ms. Jones raised four children alone, with me being the youngest. What's astoundingly interesting is that this was done with very minimal help, if any at all, from my father and never did she once complain, verbally criticize him, purposely keep me away from him, or lead me to believe that he was a bad person. This was my mother's genius of allowing me, a child, to develop my own opinion of people's true intentions. She readjusted the position that I held within the dual relationship with my father, which authorized me to see, personally, the inconsistency in his actions as well as the oral promises that never came to past. As years elapsed, I figured out that her premise for never speaking negatively towards my father was primarily, because she did not want me to lose what confidence I did have in him as a child, so that we could possibly one day form some type of bond as I got older.

Surely enough, as I got older I didn't need my mother or anyone else to tell me that my father had decided to relinquish his opportunity to be a real man, a real father to his son, but instead chose to screen himself behind scores of excuses and award false promises that never came to past. I'm man enough to admit that for years I, wrongly, held a grudge against him for all of the years of neglect, divulged lies, and the fact that he allowed my transition into an adult, the games I played while in high school and college, and more importantly, the graduations, all escape without observing firsthand. I too, interminably, carried around this grudge burden, a ton of mixed emotions, and feelings of uneasiness towards my half brother and sister, whom I love dearly and unconditionally, all because I thought they were treated a lot more fairly in the love quad, even though I knew they were not the issue. The issue was between my father and me. As a youngster transitioning through various stages of my life, in my mind, I was thinking that I was the reason for my father not giving me props that were due. There were times when I thought, "Damn, what if all of those occasions in which I sought assistance from him in relation to books for school or something athletically related, I instead, needed money to pay for an abortion, bail to be released from jail, or him to put up his house for me, so that I could remain within society—would our relationship be different?" Basically, would our relationship be firmer now if I had gone through life repeatedly screwing up? What I did know was that as a young *black* male coming from a single-parent home, the odds were already stacked heavily against me. I, too, was aware of the fact that I was going to have our white counter-parts in this world as my opposition, but the thought of having my father as my opposition as well was piercing. It seemed as if the more I accomplished in life, the wider the gap between the two of us became. After coming to terms with that certainty, I realized that the only way to close the gap was to stand in it. I vividly remember waking up one morning and conveying to God that I no longer wanted to resent my father and that I also didn't want that resentment I lugged to stop me from merging with prospective blessings or being able to bless someone else. I was then able to process and absorb the challenge as well as the painstaking metamorphosis. From that very day, I was able to see, vividly, the reasons for everything that happened. It took only twenty minutes of diligent prayer for me to stumble upon the vivacious revelation which clearly uncovered a paramount certainty—which was, all of the years of trying to figure out what I did wrong to someone else just happened to be worthless. God allowed me to see that I approached finding the solution in the wrong manner, due to false evidence appearing to be real. Despite the status of our relationship today, I genuinely respect and love my father even though there is not a sound bond between us.

I was blessed with two gentlemen in my life who shared my conscientious inner struggle and at the same time tutored my innocence as a child. One of the most valuable lessons learned from these two gentlemen was not to use patriarchal rejection as a tool to distribute hate, but instead as fuel—fuel needed to arrive at prosperity. At a youthful age, my instructions from these two gentlemen were to defeat denunciation along with America's expectations for *black* men from fatherless homes by devising a scheme that denounced prison, embraced education, and embodied intellectual strengthening. I immensely credit my two older brothers James and Tim for embracing dual roles as father figures as well as big brothers and continuously assuring me that I would one day be very successful. I must also mention that the both of these brothers are prominent fathers to their children. My sister, Jackie, also played a pivotal role in my life, adopting dual roles as my sister as well as mother figure. She always supported me emotionally and gave sound advice, even if it was not exactly what I wanted to hear. As well, I credit her efforts of making sure that I began and completed my education as a university student. As a unit we have always collectively supported one another in anything we did, be it sports, academics, or just life concerns. I have my mother and siblings to accredit for me developing into a well rounded young man that never let my father's cowardice actions broker my life.

To this very day, I honor my mother unreservedly for allowing me to see these things on my own. As she raised and cared for her four children, not once did she become paralyzed by America's expectations of a single *black* mother raising four children alone. Instead of lowering her sights, she engaged life with resilience. As if it happened yesterday, I remember my mother always stressing the importance of an education and mandating on several occasions to my siblings and I that we were, without a shadow of a doubt, going to finish high school. Two of her most memorable sayings while we were growing up were, "Welfare is for people who don't want to work," and "Aint gone be no leaning and standing." This was her way of relaying to her children that you will, without any negotiations, find something to do once you finish high school, and it will not have anything to do with the streets and standing in front of liquor and corner stores all day.

My oldest brother, James, had no choice but to become the man of the house, which meant my mother held him to a higher standard, because she knew if he did wrong, chances were, we would do wrong also. Conversely, if he made sound decisions, she knew the rest of us would follow him. To his credit, my oldest brother did do the right thing. He blazed a path that led to my older brother, Tim, going off to college. Shortly after him, my sister went, and shortly after her, I went. More importantly, every last one of us finished and not only did we finish, we all went back to college and received post secondary degrees. The point that I'm making here has nothing to do with our personal success in terms of boasting; as an alternative, I'm highlighting the fact that even though my mother and her four children may have lived in some of the most less fortunate areas of New York, Washington, D.C., and North Carolina, we all overcame the odds of poverty and became successful.

My mother always protected us from what she thought could possibly destroy our chances of becoming successful, even if we disagreed with her, and not once did she ever adopt a ghetto mentality. Furthermore, she tactically instilled strong family values and spiritual beliefs deep within us, which magnified and highlighted the power and importance of God, family, unity, and love. Still, today she says, "God and family is all you got." Even though we grew up in a fatherless home, **WE SURVIVED**, and I credit God first and foremost, as well as my mother, for every ounce of success that my siblings and I have experienced. Where have these values vanished to today though? What has happened to the belief in the things that are unseen within the homes of low-income *blacks* presently? Whether you're born in the ghetto or if it's just a pit stop for you, this should be where you become humbled by your environment and made aware of your full potential, so that you may move forward in life. The ghetto should not be accepted as a place of permanent living.

At present, it seems as if *blacks* within ghetto populations have lost their faith in God, as well as themselves, and decided to just surrender. I'm convinced that this is, primarily, due to the actuality that so many are cognitively ensnared in America within the same former times as whites who oppressed our forerunners—the exact former times that James Baldwin meticulously analyzed during the course of his existence, times which housed the unfaithful ideology that *blacks* were indeed substandard and should conduct themselves accordingly.

I periodically ride through one of the most well-known housing projects in the city where I currently live, in between edifying classes, and each time it seems as if I have entered into an alternative world—a destination one can only arrive upon as a result of travelling at utmost speeds away from the essence of *black* potential. Every single brick that makes up each unit seems to somehow articulate directly to my soul. I indistinctly hear overpowering cries of help and relinquish, as each brick represents an individual struggle and stronghold that has the entire community in a physical and mental vice-like grip. The scenery is only daunting confirmation that the mendacity which trickles off of politicians and state and city representatives tongues, words that somehow never sift to the bottom, words which have severely tainted this populace's hope, are purposely crafted stilettos for all who are victims of public school's decision to write them off, past and present obstructions, and those who were never nourished by the likes of shrewd or tangible guidance to use as a means of self-calculated suicide.

I often contemplate if the little boys who I always see on the corner mimicking their favorite athletes are aware of the unsympathetic challenges that await them right now, at a young age, and more severely as they get older. I question, too, if the parents of these adolescents have stressed to them the importance of a good education and how far it will allow them to one day advance within society, or if they have prepared these young boys to handle failure and more importantly, overcome adversity. The truth is, their innocence as children will soon fade and they will all be compelled to make decisions as young men which will affect them for the rest of their lives.

In all honesty, it is extremely difficult to make it out of the ghetto, but with faith in Jesus Christ and a watertight plan, it's more than possible. There are too many single mothers and dead beat fathers living in the ghetto without a plan and clasping to their past. As of now, the masses have not taken full responsibility for their actions. Brothers and sisters, everything that you have done that's lead to your current condition must be let go of, so that you can claim full freedom and progress away from the state that you are currently living in.

Let's face it, everyone has made mistakes in their life as well as executed bad choices that have caused setbacks, hardships, financial disparities, and pain, but at some point, we have to rebound from those mistakes, so that we can create leverage for ourselves. It's extremely important that *black* parents in the inner-city be an example for their children, because they will need someone to show them which paths to tour in life. *Black* mothers and fathers, you have to get angry, take full responsibility for your current conditions, and take your lives back. Get angry, but instead of violent consequences, transfer that negative energy into a super natural strength that will produce positive results. Again, for those who have children, you must remember how important this issue is and that this is not an individual movement, but a collective one.

The moves you make will certainly affect your children and those affects are either going to be positive or negative. Oh, and for the record *black* people, the racism crutch is now permanently broken and no longer useful. That's right! This crutch has been permanently broken and buried. Although still present, racism is no longer an excuse to be unmotivated and unproductive. Racism didn't physically position you in ghettos, the slums, and housing projects, even though it did create and implement the residential patterns which make up your localities. America agreed to residential segregation decades ago. Still, it is time that *blacks* stop using racism as a prop and start focusing on improving themselves and the problems they can fix.

QUIZ 4

- **Despite a harsh upbringing, do you believe *blacks* can still make it out of the ghetto and use their experiences as fuel to break down barriers? Why or Why not? Explain in detail.**

  _____

  _____

  _____

  _____

- **If a father/son or mother/daughter bond is broken as a result of a parent abandoning their child, is it possible for that child to still prosper? What will it take for them to excel? Explain in detail.**

  _____

  _____

  _____

  _____

- **As a product of a low-income environment, if someone does not detach themselves away from the pains and strife they have endured from their past, will they ever be able to move beyond the expectations of the "hood"? What type of effects will this have on their life? Answer with precision.**

_____
_____
_____
_____

- For someone genuinely trying to better themselves and move out of a ghetto tainted environment, is it more important for them to stay true to the "hood", the people in the "hood", or to themselves? Explain in detail.

_____
_____
_____
_____

- Is it safe to confirm that racism is no longer an excuse for *blacks* to fail and not prosper? In detail, explain your answer.

_____
_____
_____
_____

5

GOVERNMENT'S VIEW (THE POOR AND EDUCATION)

In the United States poverty and crime are drastically consuming *blacks*, especially those who are living unproductive lives and transitioning through existence without any type of tangible proposal responsible enough to permit progression. Let's begin by recognizing a simple fact. The fight to abolish them both is parallel to playing the game of chess, largely because each tactic has its strengths and weaknesses. And just like chess, using particular pieces in the exchange against poverty and crime when others should have been used could possibly cost you the game. Now, does that mean that the pieces not being used are insignificant and not board worthy? No, not at all, because every piece is necessary in winning the game; with that in mind, I must highlight the fact that the government is not a winning piece in the fight to save low-income *blacks* from poverty nor crime; instead, its uncompromising policies actually keeps them from climbing the poverty latter. Both Democrats and Republicans, alike, claim to care about this population, but caring to them only means sympathizing on cue while in town hall meetings, televised interviews, on *C-SPAN*, and when seeking support during an election term.

The truth is, the government is the principal adversary of the poor and actually keeps low-income patrons within America's ghetto communities poor with fox like strategies. As I mentioned earlier, it is no secret that this country was built from the labor of *black* slaves; despite this reality, to this day, we are still omitted from the esteemed list which relinquishes us all of the relaxed liberties to prosper from America's fruit—despite the existence of the United States Constitution. A preceding reality is that our government approved *blacks*, more so their physical labor, as only material goods in 1787 when the United States Constitution was constructed and as of today, the doctrine has on no account been comparatively modified in a fashion that extends repentance to *blacks*. This prestigious but disproportional document in which America was founded upon, when penned hundreds of years ago, was deliberately constructed with future campaigns of a colonized America, white slave holders, their families, future white generations to come, and all of their fascinations to eternally thrive, which today is why it's much more unproblematic for whites to expeditiously meet and marry opportunities, specifically those which allow them to be successful, that seem to diligently disregard *blacks*. Here, again, is why the entire African American race is continuously under pressure to survive America. As a substitute for stern restructuring, multiple guiding principles within this doctrine have temporarily been positioned to momentarily doctor and attempt to heal wounds within the *black* community which must, expeditiously, be repaired within a political sanatorium that explicitly specializes in the area of triple by-pass destitution refurbishment specifically for America's heavily populated *black* low-income localities.

Despite this prejudice scribe, we (*blacks*) have somehow found a way to maintain our sanity, but not without playing into the hands of America's reverse psychology ploy and astute plan that has hoodwinked us into believing government based programs are actually assisting those who acquire them.

RENT CONTROL

Of the many cunning tactics applied to ghetto populated areas, which on the surface appears to support and help the poor, rent control is probably the most deceiving. On paper, this ploy materializes as the necessitation that ghettos are in need of until one takes a closer look. Through rent control, landlords of properties in ghettos are forced by the government to charge lower rent rates to their tenants, but when this is carried out, the cost of **equipping** housing rises, which then lowers the monthly income of the landlords and makes providing housing less profitable for them. As a result, landlords are forced to sternly cut back on offering routine service and maintenance to their properties, which severely reduces the quality of the housing. For those oblivious of this scheme, this is the primary reason why *black* populated low-income areas look extremely run down and deserted. What good is it to propose cheap rent if the only options to reside within are of very pitiable quality? Consequently, rent control is the primary cause of what we know to be ghettos and slums.

HEAD START PROGRAMS

The government, too, favored ending *Head Start* programs. This program was initiated in 1965 with the purpose of helping ease the sting of poverty within low-income localities. Today, it primarily caters to low-income and underprivileged minority families who have preschool children ranging from ages 3 to 5 years old who are in danger of beginning school far behind their more advantaged peers. Within *Head Start* programs, children are able to develop social, cognitive, communication, and many other essential skills they need prior to entering early elementary. Furthermore, *Head Start* affords children the sustenance that a number of them are just not receiving at home: breakfast, lunch and snack. Of the many benefits of attending *Head Start*, the fact that each child's probability of repeating a grade is drastically decreased once they begin school and they are more likely to complete high school should be enough to make anyone a firm enthusiast of the program's agenda. The U.S. Department of Health and Human Services, in their *Head Start* Program Fact Sheet: Fiscal Year 2004, reported that an average per-child price tag of about $7,222 is approximately what it cost the government within a *Head Start* program. Even though this program is emphatically valuable to the low-income African American and Hispanic populations, the government, instead, voted to shift funds into the prison system which cost approximately $60,000 per inmate. Mathematically, this picture is not being painted with the goal of reaching a correct answer.

I am not against funding the prison system, but I am against ending an academic and prevention program that will have an impact on young lives and could possibly instill the necessary components that *black* children from low-income environments are being deprived of. Is it me, or does it seem more reasonable to spend $7,222 now, so that you don't possibly have to spend $60,000 in the future? If we equated this scenario to the repairing of a roof on a home, I'm quite sure it wouldn't take a home owner long to figure out which amount of money they'd rather spend and when. I hate to sound pessimistic here, but our government will likely end up spending that $60,000 on children who may possibly have *Head Start* stripped away from them when they could have likely prevented their criminal involvement by only spending $7,222. I find it outlandish that the government can find the means to print money for teenagers to go off to war and face death, but are unable to produce the funds needed to continue educational programs which can strengthen poverty-stricken areas across the country.

HIGHER EDUCATION

It is no longer a secret that the world of education has fully found itself to be a just another wealth transfer—transitioning funds from the hands of the poor to the wealthy. Colleges and Universities receive immense funding from the government, by means of all taxpayers. But even though this is happening, who is actually going to college and benefiting from this robust bursary? Among those who are wealthy, attending college is custom, a normal segment of their lives. But among the poor, mainly *blacks*, this feat is a very rare occurrence due to the academic contusions they suffer in consequence of sparring with metropolitan school systems. Aware of this prevalence within the *black* community, why isn't the government assembling educational prevention and awareness programs via education consultants who are, annually, finding themselves in middle and high school lobbies emphasizing to *black* students in low-income populations that going to college should be their top priority, as well as providing them with information that highlights funding. Instead, these same schools are getting visits from recruits representing various branches of the armed forces. So then, why are *blacks* from low-income populations not benefitting from going to college when the poor and rich both pay taxes for higher education? Is it safe to label this phenomenon as another classic wealth transfer?

BUSINESS BARRIERS

The government also implements tough barriers which prevent low-income individuals, (the select few who are even able to), from starting their own small businesses and entering the work force to capitalize on, for example, the following: lawn care, home improvement, barbershops, and beauty salons. An example of this would be the government placing sturdy stipulations on necessary paper work, getting permits, licenses, and clearances to meet zoning laws while big business decision makers just hire refined legal representatives to handle all of the amplified red tape. For the less fortunate *black* first time entrepreneur, these obstacles and the legal policies of business building could possibly be intimidating factors that keep them from progressing. Consequently, this vigorously eliminates the chances for the financially less fortunate to earn an honest and stable salary. This particular tactic is even more injurious to all of the convicted felons who have genuinely decided to turn their lives around and no longer comply with the rules of corruption. Unpleasant realities such as these are driving *blacks* to the limit of no return, which results back to what I mentioned earlier, over populated prisons. This is why we (*blacks*) must accept the fact that we will always have our backs against the wall in this dual with racial bias, but we cannot become paralyzed by this. We must continue on with multiple plans to financial freedom.

If small businesses are wiped out, the affluent are once again protected while the less fortunate are forced to remain in poverty. I personally believe if the government really wanted to help this population, they would have done so a long time ago. Again, it's no secret that the poor are poor. I am so fed up with town hall meetings being held in luxuries hotels, expensive ballrooms, and on *C-Span* that address the issues that are slaughtering *black* low-income communities nationwide. If they really wanted to help resuscitate this population, these meetings would be held directly in the communities where these brothers and sisters who need extensive help reside. In *Countering the Conspiracy to Destroy Black Boys,* published in 2004, educational consultant and author Dr. Jawanza Kunjufu wrote, "As much as I dislike Jehovah's Witnesses knocking on my door, I respect them for believing in their position and being willing to take it to the streets." Dr. Kunjufu commended Jehovah Witnesses' drive, integrity, and ability to go directly to the source of the problem in order to produce change. This is exactly what our government must do. In order to provide low-income populations the assistance that is needed to build their poor communities up, they need to take it to the streets as well. I don't know of any problem that has been, physically, fixed from afar. The immense budget used to lodge these pretentious representatives could be redirected directly into the neighborhoods that need to desperately be financially revived.

WELFARE: MALICIOUS AND DECEITFUL

Our government is completely conscious of the reality that as long as it continues keeping low-income *blacks* poor, this massive population will be compelled to be dependent upon the large scale of governmental services, remain naive to various proclamations, and easily controlled and manipulated. Controlling the masses is fuel for the government's political locomotive. The more people there are who are politically and mentally dominated denotes the immense number of individuals the government does not have to worry about voicing refutative opinions or challenging any of its arched policies in regards to its skewed implementations.

If we take a closer look at the welfare system, we will find that the entire policy was intentionally designed to control the beneficiary and do away with the *black* two-parent family home by keeping the *black* male out of the home—an act that considerably mirrors what occurred during slavery. One example that provides evidence to my assessment lies within the housing projects across America. For those living within public housing units, there are multiple restrictions placed upon them by the government and one in particular states that only a certain number of tenants can permanently occupy their units. Basically, the *black* mother is not consented to have the father of her children or any type of father figure, in any such way, living with her. As long as there is no man around, the government issued checks will continue to penetrate the premises, but as soon as a man or *black* father figure presents himself as an extension of the household, the government issued payments will immediately be threatened to either be drastically reduced or terminated. In severe cases, if this restriction is violated, they will most likely be evicted. Is it safe to assume that the government has designed a modern day scheme to clandestinely keep the *black* male out of the homes of families who are in desperate need of a *black* father figure? I do not have any concrete proof to confirm my assessment, but if one were to observe the history of *blacks* receiving governmental assistance or retrieve the results of this phenomenon from history's receptacle, they would clearly be able to see that this looks exactly like a well drawn out plan that dissects the *black* male away from his family.

In addition, restrictions are delegated to individuals receiving food stamps as well. They can only use those financial vouchers for obtaining food only. That money, in the form of a voucher, cannot be converted for the purpose of satisfying any other needs such as obtaining transportation or possibly contending with an emergency situation. I deem low-income *blacks* without any type of mental or physical disabilities who receive some type of governmental assistance, monthly, are overtly trading in their freedom for services they can acquire on their own. The government is sternly controlling a population of people who all have numerous similarities: no long-term financial stability, no education, limited life skills, and no political inclinations. By far, this is a huge audience who is unable to challenge any social injustices the government places upon them. They wouldn't even know where to begin. This ruse is the *CHAOS THEORY* at its best. Once you control a person's thinking, their actions are predictable; maybe, perchance, this is why the government has strategically knotted the entire low-income population together within every U.S. city. A cohort of hungry, struggling, financially paralyzed, self-defeated, self-sedated, and uneducated angry *blacks* all living within the same vicinity without any vision only equates to grave outcomes. How predictable is that?

"Where there is no vision,
the people will perish."
Proverbs 29:18

The government does not need to conduct a survey to find out that most individuals who are from ghetto populations do not want to be helped, are on drugs, or possibly headed to an early grave. On the other hand, this regime is also aware that a select few do want a better life; therefore, the government has created strategic instabilities and obstacles and placed them in the paths where struggling *blacks* plan to seek help. Case in point, government funded institutions that offer poverty-stricken *blacks* a chance to further their education can never seem to hire instructors permanently. Although highly qualified, the instructors within these programs are only given part-time contracts without benefits and are frequently reminded by directors that the programs are underfunded.

This type of perpetual volleying creates a very high turnover rate amongst the staff, which ultimately discourages students and causes them to quit school, only because they cannot obtain the stability they need to grow as a student. Once *blacks* become academically and morally educated, they are an immediate threat, mainly because they will no longer be able to be mentally controlled and manipulated. Again, the government is fully aware of this. Right now, *black* people, we have to wake up, pull the wool away from our eyes, and begin devising a lucrative plan of action that will allow us to move out of our fortified comfort zones and replace outdated customs and habits with more productive vigor.

The government has become the contemporary Santa Clause for the greater part of America's *black* low-income populations. Once a month, it gives a monetary gift to all who have made the inner-city roster, but that gift does not incorporate any type of information that may lead or assist them into becoming self-sufficient and productive citizens. I want to be very clear here. There is nothing, at all, wrong with receiving assistance from the government, only if it is on a temporary basis. I am totally in agreement with someone receiving assistance, so that they can transition to an elevated level of financial independency, but when one uses this form of assistance for long-term use and becomes content with living month to month on welfare, I honestly have an issue with that. It is especially sickening if an individual collecting these monthly funds is capable of working and has no physical or mental disabilities. This type of mind-set is extremely forlorn and one will never take the initiative to pursue a better life living this way.

So I ask, why allow the government to stamp you with resilient limitations and dictate how you live? Why allow yourselves to continue to remain clandestinely suppressed and a willing participant of modern day slavery, which has *blacks* cognitively and physically trapped and concealed on metropolitan plantations? Personally, I robustly suggest that the government immediately begin winging African Americans who are living on governmental assistance, today, off by phasing away the welfare system until it's completely eliminated. If there is any hope of restoring the *black* two-parent family home, it will come if welfare is eliminated and these adults are compelled to work.

It's undemanding to see that through the welfare scheme, the government has basically created cunning incentives for *black* people to willingly remain enslaved as they disregard seeking employment, education, and self-sufficiency, which only results in them remaining poor. If you are receiving a diminutive stipend each month for doing nothing and all of your invoices are fostered, what motivation do you have to enhance your personal qualities or seek employment? There are a number of individuals who are receiving government assistance and, at least on paper, they appear to be fairing far better than a number of *blacks* who are working full time forty-hour per week jobs, minus the cognitive suppression. These individuals are receiving free or exceedingly reduced rent rates, paid day care, no co-pays, and many other contributions.

Recently while out shopping with my mother, I overheard four middle aged African American women, as we all were waiting in line, engaging in a discussion in reference to their current power bill being extremely lofty. One of these women in particular seemed to have had a very nonchalant disposition as she listened disinterestedly to members of her coalition fret over their financial dilemmas. This very same woman, after listening to everyone deliberate, weighed in on the topic with what she thought was the solution that all of these women should have resulted to. This young lady replied, "My light bill was eight-hundred dollars this month, and all I did was let social services pay for it."

Because of people abusing the system, such as this young lady, is one of the primary reasons why I strongly feel the welfare system should be permanently discontinued and this needs to be put into effect immediately by, first, not accepting any new applicants and also by placing a harsh time limit and circumstances on those who are currently receiving the benefits. Furthermore, for those who are currently receiving benefits, they should be mandated to have to attend school or an institution of some sort that will give them an opportunity to further their education, budgeting, social, and job training skills, so they all will be prepared to enter the job market and the territory of financial independency once their benefit term expires. Even if the government faded away public housing, housing vouchers, food stamps, free school lunches, and so forth, there would still be support structures that would remain in place to help less fortunate *black* families until they were able to diligently support their own needs. Furthermore, all Americans receive 100% free education for their children and many other free services.

QUIZ 5

- **What are ten words that would describe someone who desperately desires to move off of governmental assistance? List consecutively.**

_____

_____

_____

_____

- **How important is executing the welfare mentality for someone trying to find a way to move to financial independency? Explain in detail.**

_____

_____

_____

_____

- Do you feel that individuals receiving governmental assistance who are mentally and physically able to work should be mandated to further their education, actively be in search of employment weekly, and be given a timely deadline to receive funds? How will these implications work in their favor? Explain in detail.

  _____
  _____
  _____
  _____

- Does the government's welfare reform truly assist low-income *blacks* or is it rewarding generational bad behavior?

  _____
  _____
  _____
  _____

- What are some advantages that work in the favor of the government of keeping the poor and needy, poor and needy?

  _____
  _____
  _____
  _____

6

SEIZE PERSONAL RESPONSIBILITY

Along with poverty issues within the inner city comes crime. With this being highlighted, would you feel safe, right now, walking at night a short distance from your house? Although crime has always been present in the ghetto, the majority of older inner city African Americans who I have recently spoken to imparted to me that they would have felt safe thirty years ago walking in their neighborhoods at night, but not in this day in time. They also stated that they did not have an issue leaving their doors unlocked all night or even falling asleep on their front porches back then.

But today, due to the escalation of drug use, a declining economy, and an increase in illegal fire arms by minors, inner-city elders exercise their right to be as secluded as possible, only to avoid becoming a victim of a random act of violence. While speaking to various elders, they also made it unmistakable clear to me that the issues which stemmed from poverty and crime within the *black* community were still present sixty years ago, but not of the magnitude of today.

I want to sober the exultation of those who feel that you can destroy crime without first destroying poverty. It would be extremely hard to argue that there is no relationship between someone being uneducated, crime, and poverty when the majority of prisoners behind bars were from ghetto populations and earned roughly *$9,000* per year before indulging in illegal activities and being incarcerated. It is impossible to defeat one without defeating the other.

Even if crime is down in a metropolitan area, poverty will still remain high. You basically have a massive population with no or very limited skills to do anything worthy of earning a lucrative income, which is heartbreaking, because most individuals within this population want to be helped, but just do not know how and where to seek it. Conversely, one must decide for themselves that they truly want to move away from poverty and do what it is necessary to permanently experience a better method of living, especially if there are kids involved, rather than depending on the government to provide for them. Remember, laziness and poverty are cousins.

> *"Nothing will ever dominate your life that*
> *doesn't happen daily"*
> *-Anonymous*

I urge all *blacks* living within poverty-stricken populations to begin taking personal responsibility for their own actions and bring to an end the blaming of society for their problems, because society is not the opposition. As I mentioned earlier, America unquestionably has its evils today, but they are not personifying themselves as horsemen draped in sheets with eye holes pierced in them or as overseers carrying whips in their hands, while relentlessly cracking them, and burning crosses all over metropolitan localities—daring us to leave unplowed city streets; the bulk of our demons are individually manufactured and located exclusively within—overpowering us from the inside out. These same demons are also ousting our belief and faith in God, our self-worth, and self-confidence. We (*blacks*) have willingly become prisoners of our own inner-hatred; and while serving these life sentences, *blacks* have found it to be exceptionally therapeutic to reprove their brethren for their current state of being and at the same time, place blame at the feet of society. I personally believe this is why, in more severe cases, our health is deteriorating at such a rapid pace, we are harming ourselves, family members, friends, unanimously rejecting education as a means of escaping poverty, disregarding authority, and continuously filling prison cells.

For years we (*blacks*) have obsessively used the blame game as a coercing bludgeon, more specifically as our own personal "Excalibur", against society and our counter-parts (whites) as an excuse not to work, quit working, and in some cases, not search for work at all, while attaching ourselves to victimization. And while in the process of using this detrimental weapon listlessly, we have wounded ourselves severely. As a result, our self-inflicted wounds have immobilized us so severely that we must now look to the same opposition who we have been swinging our swords against, for years, to help treat our injuries. However, there is certainly something immorally decadent with a fraudulent white society that has established methodologies to deposit *black* people with limited life skills and minimum education into the slums and then cunningly blame them for the transgressions produced from the depository. Nonetheless, even though blaming society and our counter-parts for your problems may be therapeutic, at that particular time, it will continue to limit you in terms of progressing.

Actually, one way to defeat your current state is to distribute your energy where it is needed the most; doing this will soon begin to produce positive results. Basically, fight battles that are only worth fighting, because sparring with society is a useless quarrel to be involved in. Instead, let's recognize and come to terms with the actual opposition, which is your self-defeated attitude and pessimistic outlook on life. I would like for my brothers and sisters to understand that all is not lost and with intense sacrifice, prosperity is vastly obtainable. As a matter a fact, it is only within arm's reach. You just have to believe it and be willing to change and make some very severe sacrifices in order to receive it. So, to all who are ready for major change, I challenge you to reflect on the direction in which you are travelling as of right now in your lives. I also challenge you to consider and reflect on the effort that will be needed to not only begin your journey from *Poverty to Prosperity*, but most importantly to finish it.

Even though accepting responsibility for your own actions is important in order to begin to solve personal problems, I do know and admit that it's not easy. It is human nature and a lot easier to "pass the responsibility", or place blame on everyone else for your failure and lack of success. There have been plenty of times in my life when I found it hard to progress, and that's when I started blaming others, blaming this, and blaming that. But as I've gotten older and grown wiser, I found that when things go wrong in my life, I can always find the culprit in the mirror. Once I honestly stopped blaming everyone else and began taking responsibility for my own actions is when I immediately became a problem solver instead of being the catalyst to the actual problem.

BLACK WOMEN MUST BE MORE RESPONSIBLE

Speaking of *blacks* needing to be more responsible for their actions, let's focus on an issue that exclusively involves *black* women. Why are you ladies allowing yourselves to become repetitively impregnated by men you are approximately 150% sure, at least subconsciously, will not be in your life long enough to help you make it through the first month of your pregnancy—once they find out that you are pregnant? Then, when the baby is born and the "baby daddy" has bailed out permanently and escaped all responsibilities without helping you support the child, you're all of a sudden shocked and feel as if he's the problem. Now, by no means am I condoning this act of cowardice by *black* men who father children and then flee the scene at the speed of sound, but with this in mind, it is imperative that I ask you ladies another question. Are these brothers solely the problem or can you women, too, find the culprit to this particular issue in the mirror? Ladies, you know as well as I do that these brothers' intentions with you were forecasted well before you became pregnant. All I'm saying is, if you see the ball coming, why stand there and wait on it to hit you in the face? I am not exercising my right to be judgmental nor am I purposely belittling *black* men, but case after case has proven that the caliber of men who are certified for this scenario are men who are all unemployed, have no long-term plans or goals, are without parental skills, have flirted—repetitively—with the prison system, or most damaging, do not encompass a secured income that's modest enough to even support a family. And despite all of these deficiencies, you sisters are still having multiple kids by men who fit this disparaging silhouette. This phenomenon enormously escapes me.

From personal observations, I have come to the conclusion that a number of *black* women aspire children, marriage, and a man so severely that they, underhandedly, allow their actions to be anxiously fueled by the nerve wrecking ideologies of pastors who ruthlessly promote finding a husband, devalue themselves, rigorously lower their standards, and ultimately go about obtaining them all the wrong way. There almost seems to be a fright amongst *black* women that they will never have long-term relationships, children, and possibly a wedding. I wonder, too, if this fear of possibly not having either of these entities to ever come to pass has become a vehicle escorting them to a world of desperate measures.

In 2009, while speaking at an assembly hosted by a nonprofit public benefit organization that makes the dream of homeownership a reality for those who reside within low-income communities, mostly single *black* mothers, I had the chance to speak with one of the single mothers, off record, in reference to the state *black* single mothers are in. She shared with me a few of her personal experiences in which she felt had hindered her in life as well as relinquished her particularized views on what she considered to be issues that were continuing to keep *black* women from progressing in the direction of prosperity. As we stood and talked, this young lady who was well-dressed actually pulled up a chair for me to sit in as if she had a lot to get off of her chest. She stated at one point, "Even though more and more *black* women, young *black* women mainly, are becoming very independent, they are still struggling to make it." She continued, "A lot of their struggles have come from dealing with sorry men that they had babies by." This young ladies definition of sorry men was *black* men who relinquished all of their rights to take care of their children.

As we continued to converse, she gave an account that was very disturbing for her. She went on to say, "I know more than one girl that tried to get pregnant by a man, because they were struggling financially and they also thought that would make the guy stick around." She continued, "And one of the guys was married." As she orated, I didn't sense that this young lady had found herself hating *black* men and women at all, but I did get the impression that she had developed, unsympathetically, very serious apprehensions with women who were devilishly mislead by selfish mind-sets to trap a man and men who refused to accept their responsibilities as fathers. So that I would not appear unconscious to the fact that women are actually pulling atrocious stunts such as this just to bait a man and look as if I thought that events such as this only happened on T.V., I attempted to maintain a facial expression that wouldn't be read as naive. I personally believe that this is one of the most self-centered acts in which a woman can succumb to. In a case such as this, the fact that a woman is so blinded by her own evil inclinations, the consequences that are sure to stem from a mishap such as this can only be toxic. Are *black* women today feeling that emotionally hopeless that they have to scheme a deceitful plan in order to preserve a relationship and keep a man in their lives or challenge another woman's shared vows in order to feel special? *Black* women, how have you ladies arrived at this dreadful destination? What's most disturbing in this entire equation is that after this tactic back fires, and it will most definitely self-destruct, the children who are conceived from this spectacle of perplexity are the ones who will suffer the most, because above all, although they are innocent, the emotional opposition they will face from the opposing family will be overwhelming, which will, at some point, cause the father to feel very little obligation to take care them. ***Oh, and ladies, just in case you haven't heard, a married man is never going to leave his wife.***

For those of you who may be unaware, one principle incentive of poverty within the *black* community is the rise in illegitimate births. *Black* women are too often making the dreadful decision of bringing fatherless babies into this world when they do not have any or very limited education themselves. Is making this type of decision being a responsible adult, more importantly, is it fair to the child? Furthermore, a vast majority of these women do not have any solid sources of income or health insurance and are only equipped with very limited parenting and nourishment skills before the child is even born. So then, let's just imagine a single *black* mother accompanied by all of these deficiencies trying to raise four, five, or even six kids all alone. The joys of child birth will soon give way to the realities of poverty and all that the ghetto has to offer. By the time these kids all reach the age of ten years old, most of them will be on a path that is routed directly for destruction, particularly if there is no father figure present in their lives.

I want to make myself unquestionably clear here. I am not suggesting, by any measures, that *black* women should abort their unborn babies who were conceived out of wedlock. My objection to this issue is that these sisters need to begin applying more responsible actions to vital situations that will gravely affect their lives by honestly evaluating themselves as individuals first and foremost and then as parents, as well as their living and financial conditions, before conceiving children. Ultimately, I also

121

strongly suggest, in reference to being responsible, that you sisters stoutly consider using some type prophylactic if you are going to continue to participate in the act of reproducing.

Black women, as a defense to dead beat *black* men and their antagonistic ambitions, when speaking on terms of one day obtaining prosperity, you must begin visualizing and seeing yourselves as self-sufficient and productive God created human beings, so that you will no longer need a man to validate your worth. I'm fully in tune with the fact that a great deal of *black* women, growing up, never received the love that they should have as a child from their biological fathers and in some cases even their mothers. That's an unfortunate reality, and it's no secret that everyone wants and needs to feel loved. Therefore, my primary suggestion to *black* women who fall into this category is that you need to immediately begin building yourselves up by honestly acknowledging and coming to terms with your emotions and current circumstances. Remember, life goes on. Stop allowing your emotional baggage to negatively influence and sucker you into thinking that you need a man, especially an unfit one, to bring you comfort. You deserve better. And for all of the *black* women who may be suffering from very severe emotional impediments due to past experiences, understand that it is ok for you to come to terms with possible symptoms or signs that signal you may need emotional therapy. Seeking therapy, even if it is frowned upon within the *black* community, from a professional or by diligently confining in a very close friend or family member who you sincerely trust to conceal what you reveal to them, in reference to your feelings, does not in any fashion signal that you are weak or demented. It actually proves that you are extremely strong and refuse to be held captive any longer by your emotions. But still, even though there are some *black* women who know that some type of formal therapy is greatly needed in their lives, a large number of them ignore it. I find this phenomenon to be heavily present in the lives of *black* professional women, even with some of my colleagues. There are numerous *black* women, young and old, who have great careers and have penetrated the upper echelons of America's boundaries, but to ease their inner struggles they are making work their lives, allowing their personalities as supervisors to run off sound potential male companions, and developing malicious attitudes as they get older, because work mode becomes their utopia.

Dr. Yolanda Brooks, a Dallas, Texas based psychologist, in 2001, spoke on this issue and stated, "Women of color tend to look at therapy as a sign of weakness." She continued, "*Black* women tend to present themselves to society as strong." Even though you may consider yourselves to be strong in a matriarchal sense, untamed emotions are even stronger. I'm absolutely convinced that if a large number of *black* women living emotive stress filled lives would diligently seek an emotional utopia, doing so would allow them to stop seeking confirmation of self-worth from men who, from the very beginning of their relationship, never sincerely cared about them anyway.

An event such as having a baby out of wedlock not only creates detrimental scenarios that will harm you as a mother, but also your child, because they will eventually become a victim of your frustrations as a result of poverty's strongholds. The outcome for a single *black* mother with limited finances, no education, and multiple children is a destructive breeding ground for her children by the time they turn ten years old, because all of the commodities they will soon be denied access to as they get older, due to restraints on her, such as well-built male regulation, clothes, material items, a quality education, and common necessities will soon make them develop a by any means necessary attitude as they look to obtain those provisions.

Mentioning that, the number of children living in poverty with a single parent is alarming. According to government statistics, 72% of African American children are born to unmarried mothers compared to 29 % of white Americans. This does not necessarily mean that these particular children do not have any type of father figure in their lives, but what it does mean is that there is a very sound chance that they do not, given the state that the *black* single parent home and *black* community is in right now. Dr. Natalie Carroll, a nationally recognized obstetrician and gynecologist who has devoted her 40-year career to diligently assisting *black* women, agrees that this is severely sad and alarming. In 2010, Dr. Carroll was quoted saying, "The girls don't think they have to get married. I tell them children deserve a mama and a daddy. They really do. A mama can't give it all. And neither can a daddy, not by themselves." She continued, "Part of the reason is, because you can only give that which you have. A mother cannot give all that a man can give. A truly involved father figure offers more fullness to a child's life." According to *Children-ourinvestment.org*, homes without fathers ultimately affect children in the following grave fashions:

- 63% of youth suicides are from fatherless homes
- 90% of all homeless and runaway children are from fatherless homes
- 85% of all children who show behavior disorders come from fatherless homes

- 80% of rapists with anger problems come from fatherless homes
- 71% of all high school dropouts come from fatherless homes
- 75% of all adolescent patients in chemical abuse centers come from fatherless homes
- 85% of all youths in prison come from fatherless homes

Not only are these children a prospect of poverty, but of crime and illiteracy also. This is so unfair to the innocent babies born into these situations, because their chances of becoming successful are slim to none before they even enter grade school. These young mothers are not even giving their children a chance when they exercise unhealthy advisability that will negatively affect their lives long-term.

BLACKS AND THEIR PERSONAL OBSTRUCTIONS

Dr. Bill Cosby has expansively been weighing in on the state of the low-income *black* community since 2004, holding what he calls "Community-Call-Outs" in cities around the country. Within these summits, as well as the book that he authored along with Dr. Alvin Poussaint entitled *Come on, People: On the Path from Victims to Victors*, Mr. Cosby does not postpone any punches as he highlights and addresses the obtuse actions that we, in particular, *blacks* who are living amongst low-income communities, continue to execute which have placed a constricted grip around the throat of the entire *black* race and severely hindered it. While in Chicago attending a community organization conference, in regards to the hike in the number of shootings that were taking place, Dr. Cosby stated, "It's just plain silly to look at what some *blacks* are doing to themselves and not see it as being just as destructive as racism." Within this particular summit, Dr. Cosby diverted the blame of the crime hike away from the actual shootings, guns, and gangs, and instead aimed the responsibility directly at the parents of these young offenders, as he declared they were parents failing to parent. In voicing his opinion on this issue, Dr. Cosby made some very essential proclamations that mainly acknowledged the fact that low-income parents are not holding up their end of the pact as trustworthy parents nor are they taking on the responsibility that many *black* leaders gave their lives for, years after civil rights decisions. Within this summit, he also stated, "*Black* parents are no longer being seen as road maps by their children, but instead they are seen as bridges that are under construction. They are failing to connect with their children because they are too busy participating in ghetto non-sense."

> *"Train up a child in the way he should go:*
> *and when he is old,*
> *he will not depart from it."*
> **Proverbs 22:6**

A few examples of the non-sense that is being practiced by *black* parents in which Dr. Cosby pointed out in his lectures are impediments such as parents allowing their children to speak unheard of dialects as a primary language (Ebonics), spending hundreds of dollars on tennis shoes and clothes for children when they can't read or write with proficiency, and not spending quality time with their children, so that they can be seen as a parent and not a stranger. In relation to reading and writing, these are not deficiencies that children can just grow out of. They have to be addressed immediately and effectively. I personally agree that all of these behaviors are outrageously irresponsible and will continue to impair *blacks* if we do not get a handle on our priorities as individuals, parents, and overall as a race. Furthermore, I too believe that instead of money being wasted on nonsense items and entities that will depreciate as soon as they are purchased, these parents should, instead, be in investing in tutors and other types of educational support for their children.

I encountered this absurdity with a parent of a student in the 6th grade who needed extensive academic help that extended beyond the classroom, while working as a Reading Specialist. The student's reading deficiency required one on one tutoring that was offered for a minimum fee, but the parent of the student endlessly used his personal affairs as an excuse not to furnish his child extensive academic help. An observable fact that escapes me is when children are in need of school supplies or extra academic support, their parents just happen to be broke, but when these parents get an urge to club, one of their friends are hit with a lengthy jail sentence, or worse, eradicated, they somehow find provisions to become financially revitalized—buying new shoes, clothes, and financing functions to keep their deceased friends memories vivid.

Another daunting issue that Dr. Cosby commented on that holds truth was the fact that *black* parents are not monitoring their children's signs of stress and unusual behaviors, until it is too late and something tragic happens. He stated, "If these parents do not bond with and gain their children's trust, they are going to be seen as a stranger and will not be able to be trusted by there their own children." His assessment on this topic is valid, because an overly relaxed relationship between parents and their children will only lead to juveniles seeking acceptance from the wrong places, and ten times out of ten, this will eventually escort children down a road filled with deadly consequences. These consequences will intensify a child's vulnerability to street deceit, which could possibly allow gangs (proxy father) and the streets (proxy mother) to easily become their surrogate parental support systems and pick up where the biological parents left off. The fact that there are not enough organizations challenging gangs, such as churches, community and youth centers, or city structured programs, the task of street recruiting is made easy. If we explore the two, gangs and the streets in comparison to *black* parents, we will be able to see why the streets are winning the battle over our *black* children.

Gangs and the Streets   Vs   *Parents*

Gangs and the Streets	*Parents*
1. Accepts the child as is	1. No longer sees child as loving once older
2. Listens profoundly	2. Proactive acts interpreted as rejection
3. Comforts/Relates to their hardships	3. No father figure available/No Life skills
4. Hours of engagement	4. Decreases bonding as child gets older
5. Promotes materialism and making money without needing an education	5. Not active in academic progress, and fails to stress the importance of an education
6. Endorses unity	6. Promotes disarray

According to this diagram, which mirrors what is actually happening within the *black* community, it is very clear to see why the streets are winning the recruitment battle of young *black* boys and girls; *black* mothers and fathers are not parenting in an effective manner and engaging in their children's lives. In the home is where rules and regulations must be set into place to guide children's curiosities and interests; and more importantly, the home is where children should feel loved and accepted the most.

Dr. Cosby, after the media released his most memorable testimony while attending a luncheon at Howard University, found himself in the middle of crosshairs and dodging shots from various angles. What I found particularly astounding was the angle from which these verbal pistols were fired. The shots that were discharged toward Dr. Cosby were not from enemy fire; instead, they came from *blacks*. Mr. Eric Dyson was one of many who fired upon Dr. Cosby saying:

> **The poor folk Cosby has hit the hardest are most vulnerable to the decisions of the powerful groups of which he has demanded the least: public policy makers, the business and social elite and political activists. Poor *black* folk cannot gain asylum from the potentially negative effects of Cosby's words on public policy makers and politicians who decide to put into play measures that support Cosby's narrow beliefs.**

It escapes me that *blacks* somehow found Dr. Cosby's comments to be offensive, as if he intentionally exercised counter-racism against low-income *blacks* or just blatantly, in the public's view, derided this population to gain some type of individual gratification. No, this wasn't the case. To Mr. Dyson and everyone else who took verbal shots at Dr. Cosby, he was simply verbalizing that it is time we begin holding *blacks* within low-income environments accountable for their current state of living and decision making, so that they will, expectantly, soon decide to make a mental as well as physical transition from *Poverty to Prosperity*. For those who are unaware, Dr. Cosby is a product of the exact same environment that he verbally lashed out against—for the sake of emotionally and cognitively inaugurating them. He was fortunate to be able to make it out and escape from the bottom of Philadelphia's most horrific slums. As well, Dr. Cosby also dropped out of high school and later went back to school and received a GED. So, who cares if he made some accurate verbal observations regarding *blacks*? My question here is, were they valid? Also, would his comments have been easier to acoustically digest and more tolerable coming from someone white? Somehow we have forgotten the premise behind his legendary T.V. series, *The Cosby Show*. Through each episode, Dr. Cosby assures us (*blacks*) that it is perfectly ok to be family oriented, cordial problem solvers, educated, live within a two-parent home, live middle to upper-class, and possess knowledge that suggest we have an unyielding handle on using grammar correctly, because these are not skills and attributes designated for white people only. We have to stop peeking at the alarming disparities in graduation rates (only 50 % of *black* students are graduating), escalating suicide rates, elevating crime and prison rates, the fact that 90% of *black* babies are born to unmarried parents, and the horrid disintegration of the *black* family unit. This crisis will not get any better nor will it fix itself. We must begin, verbally and physically, addressing the harm that we are inflicting upon ourselves and we must do it right now.

> *"If you as parents cut corners, your children will too. If you lie, they will too. If you spend all your money on yourselves and tithe no portion of it for charities, colleges, churches, synagogues, and civic causes, your children won't either. And if parents snicker at racial and gender jokes, another generation will pass on the poison adults still have not had the courage to snuff out."*
> -Marian Wright Edelman

Dr. Cosby spoke with passion when he commented on what he felt to be the some of the reasoning behind *blacks* not progressing and direction that we are headed in. It wasn't as if he was lying about the imprudent practices in which the *black* community is continuing to implement in their daily existence. Our entire population is mentally, spiritually, physically, and academically suffocating right now. How have we arrived at this remorseful point? Are we so perplexed by white society's preconceptions of the *black* race that we all of a sudden don't want to hear the truth, in relation to what's severely hindering *blacks* and keeping us from obtaining prosperity; instead, we would rather ignore what's true?

Everything that Dr. Cosby made reference to is in some form or fashion a catalyst to the results of *black* students failing in school, the increasing suicide and murder rates amongst *blacks*, an increasing dependency on the government for monthly assistance, the constant rise in the illegitimate birth rate, and the reason statistics highlight that *black* boys in America today are guaranteed to spend some part of their life locked up. I am appalled that reactions to his lecture were as if he purposely belittled and made reference to the *black* community in a manner that wasn't accurate.

In spite of all of the controversy that has spun from Dr. Cosby speaking on the state of *blacks*, I personally believe that everything he said was valid, long overdue, and needed to be addressed in the direction of the *black* community for the sake of motivating them. As well, I consider Dr. Cosby's orations to be very convincing and perceive them as a message of accepting personal responsibility for one's actions, as well as the consequences of those actions. Ultimately, what I deem to be true is that his comments were never intended to personally deride and condemn *black* parents as human beings, but to make them more aware of the chief responsibility that they are permanently committed to whether they like it or not, because as of right now, they are parents failing to parent.

QUIZ 6

- **How will attacking poverty help reduce crime rates within *black* ghetto populations across the country? Answer with precision.**

_____

_____

_____

_____

- **If someone begins to take responsibility for their own actions and make sound decisions along the way, will there be any positive benefits produced? Answer with precision.**

_____
_____
_____
_____

- How are young *black* mothers decreasing a child's chance of being successful by bringing them into their world of limited parenting skills, strife, financial anxiety, and a fatherless home? Answer with precision.

_____
_____
_____
_____

- What are some of the most essential skills that a *black* child born into a poverty-stricken and fatherless environment deterred of? Answer with precision.

_____
_____
_____
_____

- According to Dr. Bill Cosby, "*Black* parents are no longer being seen as road maps by their children." Do you agree with his assessment? Elaborate on your answer in detail. Answer with precision.

_____
_____
_____
_____

7

"HOOD" HINDRANCE

"Hood" hindrance is a toxic metropolitan dynamism which seems to plague every *black* inner-city male and female without them realizing it until it's too late. The dutiful valuing of high priced sneakers and an assortment of materialistic items which depreciate as soon as they are purchased, the love of gossip, and the attachment to the ideology of victimization are just a minority of the "hood" hindrances that are aiding in the psychological carnage of *blacks* and their inability to focus and identify the big picture that life has to offer outside of their urban citadels. These forces are so powerful that they are effortlessly deterring each *black* inner city roster in America while simultaneously untying them from society, which as a result prohibits this populace from moving away from the conditions they live within—creating the misapprehension that this type of lifestyle is normal. One major indication that this phenomenon has penetrated a person's psychosomatic realm is when animosity, enmity, and negative energy are all needed in order for them to call or present themselves. Victims of this prodigy no longer possess the necessary skills needed in order to function coherently within a non-hostile environment. Once injected into its victim, "hood" hindrance dissuades everything that reflects contentment and tranquility and cunningly pleads with love to take a back seat to hostility and anger. Case after case has proven that the mildest of conversations between its victims and those who are invulnerable from its afflictions, at some point, become merged with intolerable annotations which fabricate a key constituent that begins an intense verbal dispute. What is most hazardous about "hood" hindrance is that children are not even exempt from its monopolies and are almost certain to become victims of its results. Once they have been inflicted by this apparition, they are considered opposition to even their own parents.

"Hood" hindrance involuntary incorporates itself into the everyday lives of the low socio-economic population, only to be a replacement for what they really desire in life. The negative residue which is produced by "hood" hindrance is a direct result of the absence of three major necessities which are not instilled into lives of its victims at an early age; these necessities can be broken down into several echelons and will be mentioned in the next chapter. To *blacks* living within their self-created worlds, "hood" hindrance is viewed as a standard way of life, but for those who have escaped its grasp, it is observed as a never ending cycle that is perpetually consuming *black* inner-city populations from the inside out. "Hood" hindrance has single handedly consumed nearly every single American ghetto and has proven to be very treacherous, especially very early in the lives of children, specifically, because it painstakingly modifies their morals and values.

QUIZ 7

- Is it possible for someone to have lived in poverty so long that they reject prosperity as if it were something harmful? Answer with precision.

  _____

  _____

  _____

  _____

- How can a child that has been heavily influenced by the following be detoxified: a parent that curses regularly in front of them, continual gossip, and recurrent arguing? Answer with precision.

  _____

  _____

  _____

  _____

- Could low school performance of young *black* kids be partially blamed on their parents conditioning them to value and place more emphasis on things such as sneakers and clothes instead of academics? Answer with precision.

  _____

  _____

  _____

  _____

- When *black* parents refuse to instill the importance of doing well in school into their kids, are they exercising the "crab in the bucket syndrome" against them? Answer with precision.

_____

_____

_____

_____

- In the "hood", how effective is "Keeping IT REAL"? Answer with precision.

_____

_____

_____

_____

PREPARING BLACK CHILDREN FOR POVERTY

When parents endlessly gossip and speak negatively in opposition to one another in the presence of their young children, they are, neglectfully, providing them with vicious verbal ammunition necessary to deliver oral hardships at a primitive age. I have personally witnessed *black* parents cursing repeatedly in the company of their children and intoning obscene lyrics of songs. The moment this type of behavior occurs, parents are only validating to their children that it's ok for them to curse and use foul language where and whenever they want to, even if they, on different occasions, physically discipline them for verbally exercising distasteful language. Unquestionably, this awful behavior supports the primitive German proverb, *"The apple doesn't fall far from the tree"*, because certainly these children are not only mentally warehousing the polluted language, they're also regurgitating the same unhygienic words their parents are using within their presence, and it's happening the most at their schools.

A recent article in *The New York Times* stated that a child by the age of three, of a *black* middle class professional, had heard 500,000 words of encouragement and 80,000 words of discouragement. Among *black* children within welfare families and low-income environments, the numbers were severely depressing. By the age of three, these children had heard only 75,000 words of encouragement and 200,000 words of discouragement. The following chart provides a detailed color pattern that depicts the positive to negative word ratio between the two *black* families. As you review the chart, notice that the words of discouragement children within a *black* middle class family hear by the age of three years old, which are astonishingly low, faintly outnumber the words of encouragement that children the same age within a low-income *black* family hear.

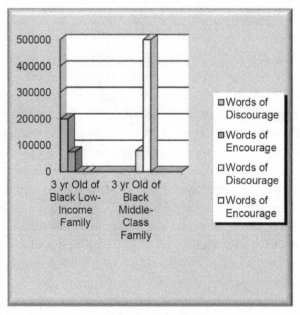

Graph by Jermaine Jones

Through the eyes of a *black* child raised within a low-income *black* family, their personal worlds are seen as a never ending place of provoking warfare where they are consistently losing battles. Hence, it's natural for a child to expect their parents to fight for their interest, but when their parents counter their expectations by using extreme profanity and all types of filthy words, not only in their presence, but in opposition to them as well, they become enormously confused. This confusion compels children to take their frustrations to a place they consider to be a perfect destination to create a war in which they feel they can actually win their schools. Since *black* children view school as a permanent place of warfare anyway, what better place is there for them to showcase an identical warrior pose as their parents while regurgitating the same filthy words they hear at home—aiming them at their peers and teachers.

In addition, this article also stated that middle class *black* parents regularly discussed with their children the value of education, how to negotiate in difficult situations, and also how to confer with difficult people. *Black* parents within low-income localities, I fail to understand why you all are not implementing these same disciplines at home and instilling them within your children. A limited vocabulary places young children at an assortment of disadvantages, especially with their counter-parts. Their word recognition ability will be extremely limited, which will place a threshold on their verbal communication skills. Even if you were neglected of these morals and values as a child, there is no reason why your kids should be denied these ethics. This should be even more of a motive to orally encourage and train your children, especially when you are already aware of how damaging it is to only be able to communicate using a minimum vocabulary and profanity accompanied by a hostile attitude. These are major hindrances that will counter children's ability to perform well, cognitively, in school on diction knowledge based test and certainly socially injure them more severely as an adult.

In the book entitled *Ghetto School*, written nearly forty-five years ago, Mr. Gerald E. Levy explored the direct connection between the *black* middle and lower class as well as the relationships amongst children, parents, teachers, and administrators. In 1967 he accepted a teaching assignment as a floater teacher which allowed him, through personal observation, to perform a case study on an American ghetto school by the name of Midway. The same unfortunate irony that was revealed to Mr. Levy then, as he analyzed the Midway School, is the exact same thing that *black* parents are doing to their children today. Just as Midway School's task became the opposite of its school's purpose, *black* parents today, instead of helping their children to escape lower class life, are instead preparing them to live within destitution for the rest of their lives. Mr. Levy, when responding to the poor attitudes in which the students of the Midway School brought into the classroom replied, "We are being conditioned to reject prosperity at home. Schools' goals are to prepare ghetto stricken children for middle class life."

This same unfortunate circumstance is, regrettably, still occurring today amongst children within low-income environments. They too are being unremittingly conditioned at home to deny prosperity and anything that relates to it. This misfortune is continually creating a major problem in terms of *black* children not being able to see further than their own personal worlds, because *black* children, especially those from low-income environments, direct tangible encounter with American society begins in school—not in their personal environments. And to add to that point, American society is going to either work for or severely work against *black* children once they become adults, so it is vital they be exposed to how America truly operates.

A major negative in this entire ordeal that is occurring within ghetto schools today is the fact that the unconstructive and pessimistic attitudes in which *black* students' homes and personal worlds are instilling in them are causing their teachers, who are living middle class lifestyles, to at some point relinquish their right to effectively reach and teach students the vital terms of success and failure, in regards to a country that already doesn't favor them. Mr. Levy found this to be true in the Midway School as well and in response to this truth he replied, "If the school systems in the hood are the vehicle for all of the ghetto lower class *blacks* to migrate, they are all headed for destruction."

As a parent, isn't a major component of parenting taking place when you are preparing your children for prosperity and providing them with the apparatus to survive America that you maybe didn't get when you were a child? Providing your children with the possessions that you did not receive as a child does not only apply to materialistic items, such as clothes and video games, but morals and values as well. These are not disciplines that are only prearranged, exclusively, for parents of a different color who possess an extensive amount of monetary leverage, or have an extended educational background. Morals and values have no price tag on them and more importantly are highly effective tools needed when raising a child.

Even if you are financially challenged, that should not be a motive to neglect being the best parent(s) that you can possibly be. A vast majority of *black* grandmothers and grandfathers alive today were poor also when they raised their children. But they will testify that they disciplined their children and instilled morals humbling, even with far less resources than today's low-income *blacks* possess. A strong vocabulary, good temperament, and the ability to negotiate are life skills that are going to play a major role in a child's life and condition them to be ready for the harsh realities that life will offer them because of the color of their skin.

If children do not obtain diplomatic problem solving skills early in their lives, as they mature into adults, even the most minor of misunderstandings are subject to transform into acts of physical or verbal violence. Now, if I'm not mistaken, the values that *black* middle class parents instill into their children are certainly values that will help shape and mold a low-income child as well, despite their position on the socio-economic scale, while producing the same results.

Lack of parenting is one of the primary explanations why *black* children today within low-income environments ethics are so distorted. It escapes me that by the age of five years old, a vast number of young *black* children know the words to the latest hip-hop songs, verbatim, how to use curse words well, and the manipulation of gang signs, but cannot read, write, nor count proficiently. This only means one thing. A massive dose of ghetto life, television, media, and the radio are taking the place of parents and playing the authoritarian's role within the household. If you were to hold a mirror up to these children's faces, you would see a vivid reflection of their parents and the environments in which they live in. This type of misrepresentation is a reflection of what's really going on at home. At the age of five years old, reading, math, communication, and social skills are vital for academic growth. Case after case highlights that the parent(s) of these students, young and old, are just sending them off to school and expecting the schools to raise, feed, and educate them, while at home, television, rap songs, and video games are taking the place of books. To the parents of children who exceedingly need help with your own academic empowering at home and can't academically assist your children, because you may not have the adequate skill sets that are needed to help them, I would like to advance the following to you as lucrative skill strengthening suggestions:

PARENTS WITH LIMITED EDUCATION

- **You must immediately go back to school and strengthen your basic reading and math skills in order to help yourselves gain leverage in the work force and to be able to help your young kids academically.**
- **Stop envisioning your child's teacher(s) as the enemy, because of their academic accomplishments.**
- **Improve your social interaction skills through community based education programs.**
- **Remember, what you did not accomplish as a student can no longer hinder you from making sure your child or children do their best academically.**
- **You must become active at your child's or children's schools and communicate *all year long* with their teachers.**
- **Preach the benefits of finishing school to your child or children frequently and what will happen if they don't. Be honest with them.**
- **Protect your investment by keeping your personal plans of prosperity separate from your friends. Everyone is not thrilled that you are trying to become a more productive citizen.**

Emotional and social distortion is forwarded to a great deal of kids in low-income populations, because the only people they have to mimic have nothing to offer them in the form of positive leadership. So naturally, young boys will be filling the shoes of the brothers in the "hood" who stand in front of the liquor store or on the corner all day, and the young girls are on deck to replace the evaporated women who have had five kids by five different men by the time they were in their late teens if *black* parents do not expeditiously change their entire method of parenting. The three major necessities in which I made reference to in the previous chapter that are missing in the lives of inner-city *blacks* are a **surplus of spiritual strength** (*the foundation*), **appropriate guidance** (*a tangible role model*), and **quality education** (*principal life skills*).

These are the frameworks that are exceedingly necessary in the initial stages of a child's life that must be implemented within the home, at an early age, in order for them to truly understand that failure, although toxic, is a choice not genetically transmissible. The home is supposed to be a place of love and peace, a place where self-confidence is built through spirituality as well as trust. It should, too, be a place that gives answers to questions that children may have, not a habitat of constant rejection. Even though you are the parent, you've got to give your child their own boundaries with restrictions.

QUIZ 8

- **Is it safe to say that the studies at the beginning of this chapter that were highlighted in the article in *New York Times* exposed the validity**

145

of why most *blacks* living on the welfare system and in public housing are not diplomatic at all? In detail, explain your answer.

_____

_____

_____

_____

• If school systems are suppose to be the vehicles that will transition low-income *black* children to a middle class lifestyle, how will this happen if their teachers have written them off and they are being taught at home to reject prosperity? In detail, explain your answer.

_____

_____

_____

_____

• Why do students in grades ranging from the kindergarten to the 3rd grade know words to multiple hip hop songs and how to use curse words effectively, but cannot spell their names, read, or do math proficiently? Answer with precision.

_____

_____

_____

_____

• How were *black* Grandmothers and Grandfathers who are alive today able to raise their children with far less resources than *blacks* today living on public assistance and still manage to instill considerably more morals and values into their children? Answer with precision.

_____

_____

_____

_____

- Why are T.V. and the environment they are surrounded by taking the place of *black* children's parents? Answer with precision.

_____

_____

_____

_____

9

THREE BOOKS-ONE ROOM

As a parent, before you continue to point fingers, blame school systems, and ridicule teachers for the failures and  academic mishaps of your children, you should first examine yourself as a leader within in your household and then pose questions that will bring forth quality answers in route to solving all of your child's academic tribulations. Parents, bear in mind, when you point one finger, three are pointing back at you. Mentioning that does not eliminate the fact that we still must continue to hold teachers and public school systems rightfully accountable in their task of academically developing *black* children. Even if, *black* parents, you may want to thoroughly begin evaluating yourselves by first questioning your personal parenting methods in reference to the rules and regulations that govern your child's homework, study time, and overall life as a student. Better yet, do you even have any rules set in place that are dedicated solely to your child's academics? There should be a routine time daily when your child rehearses their skills in the *THREE* primary subject areas which are reading, writing, and math, in addition to completing the homework from daily lessons taught at school, and this should all be concluded in your presence. Each of these three subjects should be rehearsed daily in one room. Also, ask yourself if you are providing your child with the vital tools in which they will need to develop into confident students. In a 2011 editorial published on the website *WorldNetDaily.com*, Walter E. Williams, a nationally syndicated columnist, former chairman of the economics department at George Mason University, and author of *More Liberty Means Less Government*, provided alarming specifics which pertained to *black* parents and their academic expectations in reference to their children's performance in school. Within this editorial, Mr. Williams wrote, "Here are just a few of the facts: One study asked middle class *black*, white, and Asian high school students what was the lowest grade their parents would tolerate their bringing home? Asian students replied A-minus. *Blacks* said their parents would accept grades lower than both white and Asian students."

As parents, it is your job to diligently monitor your child's academic progress annually for the duration of scheduled instructional sessions, so that any skill or academic subject area weaknesses will be able to be diagnosed and addressed within a timely fashion by providing your child the following: tutors, digital media, supplementary materials, hands on manipulatives, and technology. I am a firm believer that early parental academic interaction will help children build confidence in their own ability to learn. If a young child's parent(s) is very active early in their academic worlds and continually expresses concern in regards to their progress, wanting to do well in school will become contagious for the child. Contrary to that point, no academic interaction by a parent, within their child's academic life, will compel the child to create negative feelings about themselves as students that are also highly contagious, which will surely prove to be counterintuitive and distort their confidence to learn. These negative feelings will counter not only their initiative to want to learn, but also blemish their understanding of how important it is for them to become a well-rounded student.

A chief issue with a vast number of *black* students, today, isn't their ability to learn, but the fact that their confidence in themselves as students is severely low. This gravely hinders their performance within the classroom, and as a result, they fail to marry and concede the importance of mastering skills in subject areas that are paramount for grade-level promotion. A number of children who fit this silhouette have been told that they will never amount to anything, they're stupid, or dumb—at home as well as at school. Proof of this crisis is evident at all levels of academic learning—elementary, middle, and high school. If you were to go to either and tell the *black* students, primarily *black* males, that they are intelligent enough to get into any college or university, most of them wouldn't believe you. Here again is why parental involvement is a pivotal dynamic in children succeeding academically. Study after study has proven that parental involvement is a primary determinant of how well all children, regardless of their background, do in school. As parents, you must stress to your children that making good grades is important and then explain to them why it's important. Also as parents, you have a very important role at home to advocate, which is to assist your child in exceeding grade-level expectations year after year.

Parent's Role At Home

- Build a healthy relationship with your child's teacher.
- Create an environment that encourages learning.
- Establish a daily routine that incorporates you studying with your child.
- Monitor out of school activities.
- Turn the T.V. OFF!!!!!
- Model the value of learning through self-discipline.
- Assist as if you were their study partner.
- Read, listen to your child read, and discuss what was read.
- Praise your child for their academic success.

Childs' Role At Home

- Arrange priorities and make best use of your time.
- Ignore the T.V. and phone during homework and study sessions.
- Remain consistent, organized, and value your study sessions.
- Effectively listen in class and during homework sessions.
- Aim for mastery in reading, writing, and math through repetition.
- Avoid excuses not to learn at all cost.
- Expect to gain long-term success from each session.
- Praise yourselves when you experience small and large success as well as mastery.

Without confidence in themselves and their ability to become sufficient students, America's inner-city *black* youths will be candidates for short and long-term destruction, because as they get older, they will have to survive via a "by any means necessary" code of conduct. Living by this code of conduct in the projects and metropolitan ghettos is extremely hazardous. While functioning in this state of mind, one will do anything to make ends meet, even if it means committing crimes or even hurting someone. One thing that I am sure of is that a vast number of *black* children, today, are forced to pattern themselves, their actions, their method of thinking, and their vernacular after the only replica they have had in their lives.

It's unfortunate, but case after case demonstrates that the replica is a single mother, an older guardian, or an extended family member, who all have limited or less educational skills than they do. Therefore, these adolescents try to survive the best and only way they know how as they grow older, no matter if it's in a positive or negative fashion. Making this point, I must ask young parents a few vital questions. Why are elderly grandmothers raising your children? At what point in your child's life did you drop the educational ball? How is it possible for a five year old to get derailed away from nourishment, love, safety, and education? Prisons are being manufactured at rapid rates across the country, because African American kindergarteners from low-income and poverty-stricken areas are projected to be in the prison system by the time they are 16 years old. I'm totally aware of the fact that other races are guilty of committing crimes as well, but African Americans are leading, statically, in this area. Also, why do these *black* youth know, verbatim, the lyrics to dozens of obscene rap songs played on the radio and the *BET* network, but not the bona fide repercussions of not doing well in school or dropping out? They need to know and understand the truth that comes with not completing high school. Besides living in poverty, it is also imperative they understand, at a young age, that if they do not finish school, it's a good chance that they will one day be emotionally distressed, a victim of dire health issues, and at some time, possibly find themselves participating in criminal activity.

As a *black* educator, what's terribly painful for me to digest is that although education is a surefire avenue to success, in the "hood", it's not valued nor sought after as a means to escape that destructive and ambushing environment. Imbued with landmines, the "hood" is a massive stage play that holds daily auditions to find new *black* characters to replace those who have falling victim to crime and lengthy prison sentences. It saddens me to think that the "hood" is beginning to mirror the scenes that have been documented in the Iraq war.

I hate to be the bearer of bad news, but a sobering reality, one which is very tear-jerking, is that most *black* kids are on a path to failure and will remain on that path all because their parents are, in addition to being uneducated, so far removed from comprehending that a solid education is the golden key that will unlock so many doors for their children. A great deal of this attitude is adopted from and attached to the "hood"—an attitude that turns the cheek to book sense and encourages young *black* children to sabotage their futures by yielding to penitentiary bound hallucinations. For *black* children, this is an alternate form of suicide and for the parents of these children, they should all be charged with felony academic homicide. These parents are so ensnared in their self-created worlds that they have failed to come to terms with the cruelness their child will be up against if he or she does not receive the proper education that is necessary to progress in society. A large majority of a child's academic knowledge base is learned long before they are ever enrolled into any school. Children learning their ABC's and the sounds each letter makes (phonemic awareness), articulating and forming sentences, improving writing skills, and building a strong vocabulary should be completed at home, at the kitchen table, so when they do enter school, they will be ahead of the game.

Speaking of building a strong vocabulary, the SAT and other standardized test that evaluate academic validity is where a large majority of *black* students are failing. While visiting a predominately *black* 8th grade class in Durham, N.C. to place emphasis on maintaining strong grades in order to be able to go to college, I asked the entire class if they knew what a (Toboggan) was twenty minutes into engaging in conversation with them, and 100% of the class immediately said, "A hat!" After I explained to them that a toboggan was not, at all, a hat but instead a device that is used to maneuver around in the snow, these students were in complete disbelief. Of course, many of them did not believe me until I had the teacher issue each student their own dictionary, so that they could see for themselves. Their definition of the word toboggan was conceived from their environments away from school in addition to what they had been told all of their lives by their parents. Is it safe to assume that the parents of all of these 8th graders were unaware of the accurate meaning of this word as well?

As I pose this question, my purpose is not to deride any of their parents, at all, but to instead make an attempt to pinpoint exactly where the setback, in terms of vocabulary awareness, lies within the homes of *blacks*. So then, if these parents were aware of the meaning of the word toboggan, why hadn't they disengaged themselves away from the use of the fabricated meaning that *blacks* have created and instead married themselves to its authentic meaning for the sake of educating their children? Is it safe to assess that these parents are too victims of academic slothfulness? In a perfect world, schools will be preparing *black* students for the SAT by the time they reach the 3rd grade, but unfortunately, this is not the case. A callous reality is that the vast majority of America's public schools only concentrate on a curriculum that mirrors that of the Standard Course of Study, or better yet, teaches what the government obliges them to teach. This is what I refer to as "compelled instruction". In reference to *black* children, SAT prep must begin with parents and their children sitting at the kitchen table as well. This is one primary reason why parents have to provide their children with the educational repertoire they will need within the comfort of their own home, because public school systems are neglecting to do so. Parents, instead spending money on expensive and non-tangible materialistic items, that money needs to be invested in tutors, phonemic awareness modules, and after school programs.

> *"My mind is my modern day spear"*
> *-Nas*

In line with *black* children needing to develop a sturdy vocabulary, parents, you all must begin as early as possible with preparing your children for the development of excellent orating skills as well. Stress to your children that "Ebonics" is indeed a large aspect of the *black* culture, but it is not what standardized scholastic test will evaluate them on. These tests severely reject cultural terminologies and dialogues. The downplaying of these critical scholastic elements is convincingly leaving *black* kids at the academic starting block, while the winners, our counter-parts, are celebrating at the finish line. The negative attitude that *blacks* have been carrying for years towards being educated must be reversed instantaneously in order for our children to avoid the malicious results life hands uneducated *blacks*. The importance of good grades has to begin to be instilled into children's heads early by their parents, even if they have to explain the truthful harsh realities of what will happen without them. As a matter a fact, go ahead and explain these hard truths anyway. Again, it's depressing and unfortunate that within low-income *black* families, today, academic success is not being highlighted and praised as the route to take to earn a decent living. Instead, eating from the streets is what's given admiration.

At home is where books should be provided for the older children in the household to read to younger children. This will condition children, while in grade school, to want to learn more and strengthen their reading and vocabulary skills also. Furthermore, *black* parents you have to be involved in your children's academics daily and stop letting them tell you that they do not have any homework after school or on the weekends without raising any questions. More importantly, these students must be supported throughout their entire academic career, not just in primary grades—kindergarten through 3rd grade. Parents are decreasing involvement around the end of 3rd and the beginning of 4th grade. This is the primary reason why the *black* community is falling behind in the area of end of grade (EOG) testing and the children are being recommended to be placed into special education classes when they do not need to be, losing interest in school, and more severely, ending up in the criminal justice system. Additionally, parents are just going along with their child's school curriculum and didactic standards set forth by their state and the government, even if it conflicts with their child's learning style. We have to stop allowing institutional racism, which teaches *blacks* to be schooled and not educated, blindfold us and our children from this point on.

> *"Education is the most valuable thing that*
> *you can acquire in life"*
> *-Rapper, T.I.*

These major shortcomings that parents are exhibiting are rapidly causing young African American students' grades and standardized test scores to suffer. There are just not a enough hours in a day for teachers to teach, raise, counsel, and emotionally support students as if they were their own children. Parents should be providing their children with these assets at home. A major issue that I have with a great deal of *black* parents is that they are not even taking the liberty to personally visit schools periodically to check in on their children and make sure that they are doing what they are suppose to be doing.

Placing the multiple responsibility hat on top of teachers' heads, as well as school systems, creates an overwhelming burden for them both to carry and exemplifies the academic neglect that each *black* child is experiencing at home by their parents. *Black* parents have somehow found a way to see their children as everything except good quality students. This is one of the chief reasons why it's extremely difficult for teachers to get the parent(s) of their students to show up and meet with them at their schools, in reference to their child's or children's academic progress. In the book entitled *Me Teacher, Me . . . Please!*, published in 2002, Educational and Management Consultant Dr. Wilbur Brower gave attention to several basic responsibilities that parents must carry out early on in their children's academic development. The responsibilities that Dr. Brower referred to in his book are as followed:

- **Parents must demand respect from their children, and show no disrespect to teachers. I've learned that when parents bad-mouth and disrespect teachers, children are inclined to also.**

- **Parents must invest in their children's education. One way of doing this is by getting them involved with culturally/socially significant activities, buying educational materials, giving them educational experiences, subscribing to educational materials such as magazines, video etc. I often said that many parents spend more money on beer and cigarettes during one weekend than they spend on their children's educational exposure during a whole year. When they send their children to school wearing the latest fads and fashions, but do not ensure that they have paper and pencils, it is a statement about their values and what they expect of and from their children.**

- **Teach them a sense of personal responsibility. Children must learn from their parents that they are responsible for their successes and failure; and that they will be held accountable of their behavior and their choices. When parents constantly bail children out of predicaments they get themselves in, the children will learn**

that their parents will come to their defense, even when they are wrong.

- **Parents must understand that the paths their children take is determined, to a large degree, by their actions and behaviors. Children will seek their own identity and rebel against many things we hold sacred and value. That's all a part of their growing up. But, participating in and re-enforcing their self-destructive behaviors is a form of suicide for children, and homicide by parents!**

The inconsiderate promotion rate and low AYP scores within schools that accommodate predominately low-income *black* students prove that two chief motives primarily responsible for a large majority of *black* parents showing up to their child's school are if they are told another teacher or student has unsympathetically mistreated or put their hands on them or if the child is in great danger of repeating the same grade. Case after case has proven that commonly at that point, it's too late to help the child, because the academic school year is nearly over. From personal experience working as a Reading Specialist within a charter school that mainly catered to low-income *blacks*, I know firsthand that once most inner-city students leave school, their academic learning stops.

When my students returned home from school, no one within their households were reinforcing any of the skills or lessons that were taught previously that school day. Students, ranging from kindergarten to 3rd grade, would leave school, come back the next day, and frequently tell me that no one at home helped them with their homework. Surely, initially, I didn't believe them; therefore, on random occasions I contacted parents and guardians, those who supplied valid contact numbers, of each student to validate if what their child was saying was true. To my surprise, each child was in fact telling the truth. Every parent I contacted had an excuse to why their child was not getting academic support at home. If this was happening for an entire school year, how much were these students really learning while at home and more importantly, retaining by the end of the year? That's right, not much at all, if anything, and their end of the year test scores revealed it.

As well, a great deal of parents are not even promoting to their children the good that will come about if they at least graduate from high school and how finishing will greater their chances of not having to live in poverty, depend on the government, and have to work dead end jobs. *Black* parents are totally unaware of the fact that failing to academically support their young children is only preparing them for poverty.

QUIZ 9

- **Should teachers be held accountable for children who fail, because the skills that are being taught in the classroom are not being reinforced at home? Answer with precision.**

  _____
  _____
  _____
  _____

- **What type of message are parents sending to their children when they send them to school with designer clothes and the latest fashions, but** do not assure that they have all of the necessary books and materials they will need to pass their grades? Answer with precision.

_____

_____

_____

_____

- Are middle class white teachers doing a good job of relating to and teaching inner-city *black* children? In detail, explain your answer.

_____

_____

_____

_____

- How important is it for teachers to be able to relate to students who are coming to school from impoverished environments? Answer with precision.

_____

_____

_____

_____

- Do you believe an increase in more *black* male teachers will help deliver *black* students from the academic destination they are currently in? Answer with precision.

_____

_____

_____

_____

10

EDUCATED BLACKS ARE NOT YOUR ENEMY

The paradox that education is an entity which is limited to primarily white people has been accredited by *blacks* living within the ghetto for decades. Through their eyes, education has been regarded as a method for only white people to become self-sufficient and prosperous. As well, within low-income populations, an individual who's believed to be educated beyond the realms of what the "hood's" curriculum offers is often misunderstood and observed as an alien by the majority living within their environment, because one being educated contradicts "hood" ethics. By and large, if an African American speaks proper English in the "hood", they are instantaneously labeled as "sounding white." An asset such as being able to verbally express yourself by having proficient dominion of Standard English has somehow become coined as being "Booshie" within the *black* community. I'm fully aware of the fact that there is nothing at all dumb about those who speak *Black* Vernacular English, as linguists call it. I also understand that it is just another dialect that some may consider to be just as valid as Standard American English, Southern English, New England English, British English, Australian English, or Singapore English. Even still, I have a motto in which I intensely believe in and relay to all of my students within each advanced English class that I edify, which is, "Being able to speak English correctly is similar to having insurance on your vehicle. It's better to have it and not need it than need it and not have it."

In a recent column entitled *I Don't Speak White*, posted on *www.Times.com*, Taylor Ivana Trammell, a senior at Detroit's Mumford High School, weighed in on the tough experiences she faced with friends and going to school as an African American who was groomed, from childhood, by her mother to speak proper English. Taylor said:

> I was not accepted as *black* among my friends. The language I used was just "too proper" to be "*black*". That's just sad. It's just hurtful to think that my generation does not believe that using proper English is the way *black* people should be speaking. What is strange about speaking English correctly? If I am educated, why should I speak as though I am not? I am *black*, and the way I speak is neither *black* nor white. The way I speak is intelligent. I finally accept the way I talk. All people, no matter what race they are, have the capability to speak their language correctly. When my generation realizes that it is not wise to look upon intelligent speech as a shortcoming, then maybe the practice of using poor speech will end. Here's what

my African American generation does not realize: When they say I talk white, they're stating that they themselves don't have the ability to talk proper.

Not only does speaking properly spark envy, but if *blacks* living within low-income environments decide to move out to create a better life for their families and move into an improved environment, they too are immediately labeled "Booshie" by those who remain amongst the setting. I have more to say in reference to this ideology, but before I go any further, I would like to ask a simple question. Just what does the term "Booshie" mean, more so when verbally fired in the direction of and used in a manner to illustrate *blacks*? Despite the obvious or, better yet, what the Urban Phrase Book tells us its meaning is, does it by any chance— in relation to *blacks*—reference those who pride themselves in operating outside of a world of amplified gum smacking, one not habitually using the overwhelming use of broken English for the sake of not knowing how to systematically construct sound sentences, someone who desires to think outside of the box, and those who have detached themselves away from victimization?

I'm reminded of an incident which occurred when a very good female friend of mine, in trying to justify why she did not want to socialize with two other close friends of mine who just happened to be married, labeled them both "Booshie", even though she considered them both to be cordial associates. Initially, this comment made me very furious and defensive on their behalf, because this fairly young married *black* couple had never given me the impression of being anything remotely close to term "Booshie". As a matter a fact, I always thought, since the first time that I met them both and still to this day believe, that they are just quality young *black* individuals who are striving to survive America and value their education as well as see themselves as products of an environment that could have swallowed them whole. In fact, it was both of these individuals' prior environments that compelled them to take advantage of an academic escape route out of the "hood". Later that evening, still feeling a bit livid, I began to thoroughly search for possible reasons why this young lady would make such a judgmental and illogical comment about these two really good friends of mine, particularly because she is a product of the same harsh environment as the both of them. As well, she too obtained a college degree, minus the actual traditional on campus college experience.

Days later, after sternly executing cognitive diagnostics of the premise for her making that comment, I was finally able to put my finger on the hypothesis which fueled her words. This young lady's perception of *blacks* living a middle class lifestyle in America had been brutally smeared by the same world she is a product of—a world that she has yet to mentally escape and is also exempt of *blacks* possessing middle class values.

Being raised by an older extended family member, morally she was instilled with great ethics and values; unfortunately, though, cognitively she was injected with a high dosage of outdated ideologies that left her socially bankrupt and unaware of all of the tools she would soon need in order for her to survive America. This young lady failed to shed off the old-fashioned methods of thinking that have hindered her from functioning proficiently outside of a de-escalated conversation as well as socialize within a high profile social colloquy, failed to successfully unearth the importance of not only obtaining but securely understanding the value of a quality education, neglected to understand the importance of making herself marketable, and abandoned acquiring the necessary proficiencies needed in order for her to be able to converse within the presence of an assembly of *blacks* who are immune to the sting of old-fashioned methods of thinking and have obtained a college education.

For a vast majority of the older *black* generation still alive today, chiefly those who are products of Southern states such as Georgia, Alabama, North Carolina, and Mississippi, the idea of obtaining an education, at least doing so uncontested, was a proposal they were never able to earnestly flirt with; despondently, the peephole from which they view the world lucidly suggest that educated *blacks*, today, are people who they have nothing in common with and in a large number of cases insinuate that these prevailing brothers and sisters, via their academic feats, have been equitably disconnected away from the plights of the lower class. Essentially, forerunners today deem *blacks* who are educated, for some peculiar motive, wear their accomplishments on their sleeve and function as if they are more meaningful to America than those who are uneducated.

Functioning under unfashionable theories, within this young lady's personal world, it is not educated *blacks* who perplex her; it is more so what they represent, in addition to their individual qualities: people who are well spoken and able to verbally conduct themselves in a manner that highlights knowledge and counters ghetto slang and someone who understands that the environment that groomed them did indeed influence them a great deal, but that same environment also had to be disengaged away from their mental repertoire, at some point in their lives, in order for (the big picture), which is long-term growth and well roundedness, to materialize. These qualities represent everything that she has not yet obtained, only because she declined to escape the world that cognitively groomed her. This dark world that she has confined herself to has socially and psychologically paralyzed her so severely that she has no desire to connect with anyone outside of her realm who does not share the same out dated cognitive qualities that she does. In fact, this method of thinking has managed to offer her no exemption from seeing the world through anything less than a blurred peephole's view.

GHETTO EXODUS

First, *black* men and women, recognize and understand that leaving the "hood", cognitively or physically, is not a bad thing at all and in actuality, leaving the "hood" will be one of the best decisions that you will ever make at this point in your lives.

A vast number of gangsta rappers have glorified violence, killing, jail, and staying in the "hood", no matter how much money they have, so frequently within their music that the very people the music influences the most have actually bought into this forged ideology and trust that is what they should do. This only confirms that *blacks* are afraid that abandoning the ghetto lifestyle will discontinue their chances of being popular and accepted by their environment as well as blemish their potential street creditability. But a sobering reality is that this insincere ideology has no merit beyond the walls of their citadels. The last time I verified, being liked and accepted amongst friends did not pay any bills nor did it put food on the table.

One goal of leaving the "hood" is to one day have an individual be able to come back to the same environment that they made it out of to help someone else move ahead of that population. This will certainly be exercising God's "Steal Sharpens Steal" philosophy. I understand, too, that not all of the unprivileged within America's arduous ghetto citadels desire to be helped, and that these outsized number of individuals are perfectly content with how they are living. That's very unfortunate, but it's the nature of the beast. With all due respect, those are the individuals who you just cannot spend time trying to continuously save, especially if they do not want to save themselves.

> *"To master the world, you must know the world, hence you pass outside of your own district, of your county, of your own country, to know the world and possess it because all that is in it is yours for the getting, go out and get it."*
> *-Marcus Garvey*

Recognize, though, that moving away from the "hood" invites room for one to be publically disdained by those who remain an ingredient of poverty-stricken populations. But an individual is highly endorsed and accepted amongst the ghetto congregation if they have multiple kids by multiple men, go to the same club every weekend, are always looking for the get over, or struggle just to get by day to day without a job and steady income. This cognitive foolishness is evidence that *black* racism is exceedingly germane and greatly exercised within the *black* culture. *Blacks*, for some strange reason, exercise the same racism amongst one another they condemn whites for implementing. Not only is skin tone and education dividing *blacks*, but so is success, both small and large achievements. Although outlandish, this is what's actually taking place within the *black* community.

For the few who decide to seek academic help, despite their age, through literacy centers, community colleges, or any other institution that will allow someone to receive a GED, Adult High School Diploma, or even a chance to just further their basic learning and life skills, they're considered an outcast. This is a phenomenon that *blacks* somehow seem to be magnetized to. In *The Envy of the World*, author Ellis Cose explored this same cultural blemish while giving his account of a young man by the name of Mike Gibson who he conversed with in December of 2000. In Cose's conversation with Mike, the young student stated, "Certain members of my family put me down for going off to college, tried to make me feel guilty for leaving." Despite the negative energy aimed at him by his family, Mike still managed to succeed by graduating from college and escaping destructive ideas. With the help of a mentor, he was able to triumph and change his life around in spite of growing up with a drug addict mother, a father who was never around, and constant violence in his neighborhood.

Just as Mike, I too experienced envy from certain family members when I went off to college. A great deal of this envy was expressed non-verbally, via their gestures, whenever I came around. But as far back as I can remember, a number of these particular family members have always, for some apparent reason, been envious of my siblings and me, more so our accomplishments, as well as the paths that we have chosen to travel in life, despite the fact that we all come from the same family origin; basically, we all come from the bottom. Still today, when I am in the presence of these particular family members whose goals were not the same as mine, who chose not to use education as a tool to reach prosperity, whose lives have now peaked out because of the choices they have made, and who also didn't make a conscious decision to leave their old world's behind, I bid them all well, but I still sense an unwelcoming aura which confirms that they are, unfortunately, still and will always be tied to a mutual obligation of envy from which they are unwilling to break free from.

After personally speaking to individuals who were experiencing this same type of betrayal from their families and friends, I found it imperative to offer them strong words of encouragement. They were really wedged between pursuing a better life and remaining an active member of a needy population, just to satisfy the selfishness of others. I spoke from the heart and I told them, "Without an education, communication, and job skills, your chances of survival in this society are slim to none and as a result, the government will become your source of dependency for the rest of your lives." I gave these individuals something that no one has ever given them before—the truth. For some strange reason, there is a horrid spirit of envy aimed towards those seeking success and detachment away from governmental dependency by those who are just riding the system out within low-income African American inner-city populations. Being educated can no longer be frowned upon and devalued. Listed below are just a few of the long-term effects of dropping out of school:

THE HARSH REALITIES OF DROPPING OUT OF SCHOOL

- **National Data. Students from low-income families are 2.4 times more likely to drop out of** school than are children from middle-income families, and 10.5 times more likely than students from high-income families.

- Health Issues. Dropouts are more likely to have poor health.

- Public Assistance. High school dropouts are also more likely to receive public assistance (Welfare) than high school graduates who do not go on to college. In fact, one national study noted that dropouts comprise nearly half of the heads of households on welfare.

- Single Parents. This increased reliance on public assistance is likely due, at least in part, to the fact that young women who drop out of school are more likely to have children at younger ages and more likely to be single parents than high school graduates.

- Prisons. The individual stresses and frustrations associated with dropping out of school have social implications as well: dropouts make up a disproportionate percentage of the nation's prisons and death row inmates. One research study pointed out that 82% of America's prisoners are high school dropouts.

I wholeheartedly believe that if *blacks* who have made it out of poverty and obtained some degree of success would just go back into low-income communities and model success, those who are willing and desire to truly be helped will follow and allow these individuals to show them how to further their education and acquire the life and job skills they have not yet obtained, but are necessary and needed in order to survive in America today. All this population needs is to be shown how; and by showing them how, those who have flirted with success will be in tune with Lao Tzu's ideology of world management. *"Give a man a fish and you feed him for a day. Teach a man to fish and you feed him for a lifetime."*

QUIZ 10

- **Do you believe that the hatred and envy in which *blacks* have embedded deep within are genetic deficiencies caused by the traumas of slavery? Answer with precision.**

  _____

  _____

  _____

  _____

- **Are *blacks* afraid of detaching themselves away from an impoverished lifestyle, because they have not established their own identity? Explain in detail.**

  _____

  _____

  _____

  _____

- **How is it that *blacks* oppose racism from whites, but apply the very same prejudice against individuals within their own race, especially those who are educated? Answer with precision.**

  _____

  _____

_____
_____

- From personal experiences and through personal observations of your family members and friends who chose to abandon education, how important is obtaining an education to you? Explain in detail.

_____
_____
_____
_____

- Why is education viewed as the "white mans way out" to *blacks* living in poverty? Answer with precision.

_____
_____
_____
_____

11

BLACK MEN, LEADERS OR COWARDS??

While I was working as a Reading Specialist in 2006 within the Charter School system, Dr. Wilbur L. Brower made a powerful statement to me while attending a state wide conference entitled *African American Males in Education.* He told me, "A setback is a setup for a comeback." The words Dr. Brower spoke had multiple meanings. They primarily played dual roles, providing me with the wisdom and strength I needed at that particular time to remain encouraged as a young *black* educator and leader within the classroom. Subsequent to that conference, I realized how important it was for me to stay on the path of becoming a leader as well as taking on the duties and responsibilities that come along with the territory of being an instructor. I immediately began to envision myself as a figure that would one day be able to lead collegiate students to academic success in the classroom as well as be an insightful mentor to young *black* men who were products of the same trials, tribulations, and environment as me.

Today, within all of the classes that I instruct, as a part of what I like to call "Building Sessions", I strategically engage in various discussions with my male students, so that we can better understand one another's view points on various topics. I initiate these sessions, because I have found that men have a tendency to gain a great deal of respect for one another when they open up and speak from the heart. One of the topics that always seems to make us run over our thirty minute allotment is the importance of a child, particularly a *black* child, having a father figure present in his or her life. The entity in which all of these men seem to always be in agreement with, above all topics, whether old or young, is that fathering children and not taking care of them has become such an out dated, lame, and overachieved practice. These feelings are mainly bred from the relationships that these men never had with their fathers.

In addition to numerous issues and a self-defeated mentality, I believe that a great deal of *black* men can't progress in life, because the majority of them are not doing or have not done right by their children. I used to believe that every *black* man, at some point in their lives, dreamed of being a great father. If that is remotely true then I must ask the following questions. How can a man look in the mirror at himself knowing that he is an unreliable father, because an unreliable father is just the same as an absent father? How does one come to terms with abandoning such a delicate investment? How could a man use the relationship that he has with his children's mother as an excuse not to take care of his children? This epidemic involving *black* men relinquishing their rights to be unswerving fathers to their children has become such a widespread problem that even President Barack Obama, initially when seeking office, weighed in on this issue demanding that fathers, chiefly *black* men, bear the responsibility of healing broken families. President Obama castigated absent fathers when he professed the following:

> **Black men have abandoned their responsibilities, acting like boys instead of men. You and I know how true this is in the African American community. Outlining statistics show that more than half of all *black* children live in single-parent households. Such children are five times more likely to live in poverty and commit crime, nine times more likely to drop out of school, and 20 times more likely to end up in prison. And the foundations of our community are weaker because of it.**

During the horrific events of slavery, *black* mothers and fathers were forced to abandon their children to satisfy the demonic and selfish desires of malevolent captors. The pain of separating from their children was so brutal that a vast number of *blacks* eventually committed suicide and some even went as far as to kill their own children to avoid being disconnected from them. Dr. Vernon McClean, a Professor of African American Studies at William Paterson University, in a recent essay, *Black Fathers, Invisible Men,* underscored the fact that slave narratives reveal that African American fathers who were enslaved were extremely nurturing and caring fathers to their children. To support his assessment, Dr. McClean referenced a book entitled *Roll, Jordan, Roll,* written by Eugene Genovese in 1978, in which he related the story of a Virginia slave who actually chopped off his left hand with a hatchet to prevent being sold and separated from his child. As well, City University of New York Historian Herbert G. Gutman in his book, *The Black Family in Slavery and Freedom, 1750-1925,* spoke on the unconditional love that *black* slaves, especially men, had for their families. Within his book, Gutman quoted a Natchez, Mississippi slave overseer who said, "Slaves who outran the owners' dogs would usually stay in the vicinity and risk recapture to see their families again."

> *"It's time for us men to say to ourselves, I am more interested in raising my child than any issue I had before. I'm going to behave or get help, but it's about the child"*
> *-Bill Cosby*

Mentioning these events, how did an immense number of *black* men, today, arrive at such a sorry destination in regards to parenting? It is a disgrace to see that so many *black* parents, mainly *black* fathers, are exercising their right to be overly unreliable and in more severe cases, just disconnecting themselves away from their children alto-gether without a trace—at the speed of sound. Parenting is not a commentary sport. Everyone, meaning both parents, must be in the game, because it takes a team to raise children appropriately. Children, both boys and girls, need concrete leaders in their lives from day one. They need someone they can physically touch who is travelling on a road of positivity, or at least someone who will be able to keep them focused. Without making light of the importance of a young *black* male having a father in his life, this epidemic is even more monumental for *black* men who have daughters. Although mothers have a very secure bond with their daughters, the father is the one who shapes his daughter's identity as she transitions from an infant to a woman. By shaping a daughter's identity, I mean the father is the one, between the critical years in his daughter's stages of maturity, who has to instill in her that she is beautiful, she should never seek a man's approval to justify her worth, and that her brother should nurture, love, and take care of her as if he is her father. Additionally, as a father, you will be the first man your daughter will have to employ as a blue print of how a woman should be treated; and from this blue print, she will one day be able to make a clear distinction between the good and bad intentions of a man. Oh, and I must also mention that the hate in which daughters develop over the years for their unreliable or absence fathers will remain in their hearts forever.

ROLES OF A FATHER IN HIS DAUGHTER'S LIFE

- Show her unconditional love.
- Model the role of a successful man.
- Teach her how to value and respect herself.
- Instill values in her, so that she will not need a man to validate who she is.
- Be a person of value for her.

As they grow older, one of the most important necessitates that children will need is advice, and this advice will need to come from someone who has been very influential in their lives. Again, I am not by any means making light of a mother's role or her ability to be a sound leader within the relationship she has with her children.

I just firmly believe that a man is equipped with more effective tools that are needed to ultimately defeat the "Evil" we are up against.

A large number of fathers may not agree with me, but I sternly believe that your children possess the right to question you regarding your lack of parenting, particularly if you are not doing your job as a father. As I specifically target dead beat fathers, it's not my intention to minimize the efforts of all of the real fathers out there who are embracing their responsibilities as fathers as well as providers, whether they are amongst the homes their children live in or not. Making that point, I ask that *black* women continue to support these brothers who are stepping up to the plate, regardless of the status of your relationship with them. Allow these men to continue to provide for their children and while doing so, compliment these brothers and commend them for being real men. In Dr. Vernon McClean's article that I referred to earlier, *Black Fathers, Invisible Men*, he also advanced seven sound suggestions that others can do that will be helpful in supporting *black* fathers who have accepted the responsibility as a provider:

1. **Reach out to *black* fathers. If you know a full time dad, give him support, let him know you care and encourage him.**
2. **Take your brother/Father to a church, synagogue or mosque.**
3. **If the *black* father has been abusive, use the occasion to help him discuss the situation.**
4. **Boycott radio stations, talk-show hosts, newspapers, and businesses that defame *black* fathers.**
5. **Oppose further cuts in jobs and social service programs. Defend those programs and policies**

that allow *black* fathers to earn the money necessary to provide for their families.

6. Encourage "full-time dads" to join a *black* men's group, such as those organized in the inner cities. *Black* men need the support of other *black* men in order to be good fathers.

7. Encourage teachers and professors to discuss the plight of the *black* father in their classes.

While these are first-class suggestions, I want to turn the focus of attention back to all of the fathers who have abandoned their children and given in to their own selfish and self-fulfilling prognoses.

These men are no longer able to see the validity in being a leader, short or long-term. But guess what? All of the neighborhood drug dealers, gangs, and underhanded cormorants disguising themselves as leaders are just a minor number of those who are impatiently waiting to reveal to your children what their connotation of guidance is all about; and just as Satan, they are continuously eying new recruits.

> *"Or what man is there of you, whom if his son ask bread, will he give him a stone? Or if he ask a fish, will he give him a serpent? If ye then, being evil, know how to give good gifts unto your children, how much more shall your Father which is in heaven give good things to them that ask him?"*
> *Matthew 7:9-11*

As a matter of fact, they are all instructing classes on leadership (101) and the valuing of non-tangible substances in the streets (102) as you read, but these leadership classes do not involve escaping America's invisible chains or acquiring the knowledge that is needed to transition from *Poverty to Prosperity*; instead, these courses teach short-term and misleading information that is going to surely prepare them for prison or worse, death. These courses, too, are purposely structured around a curriculum that presents false methods of accomplishing in life in a manner that appears real. What is even more deadly is that these particular courses offered from these surrogate groups are, all, keeping *black* children ignorant of how the real world functions along with depriving them of the tools they will need to survive within it. Male parental leadership is greatly needed in the lives of young *black* children, so that the gap between right and wrong can be bridged.

I personally do not see this petition, (children questioning their fathers about their parenting skills), as an act of disrespect or insolence. I simply feel that if children can't make a trustworthy connection between what their fathers are instilling in them and the real world, more specifically, this distorted society that we live within, then they have a right to question their skills as parents. It's not even worth saying to these cowards, "If you didn't want children, you should have used protection." That would just be a waste of oral energy. It's time for all dead beat fathers to begin helping support their children and the single mothers raising them, even if they are not living within the same household. As for the brothers who are living amongst the household, it is important that you all begin doing a better job of taking care of your families and stop functioning as if you are allergic to manual labor. In the struggle for labor equality, there is no time for a pride parade.

Let's be honest here brothers, in comparison to your counter-parts, you are at a great disadvantage. The tools in which you currently possess, (over all academic muscle, a regulated temperament, articulation, networking, worldly awareness, and over all people skills), to compete against the opposition, (our white counter-parts), within society as of right now do not compare, at all, to what they are already armed with.

Mentioning that, understand that these tools are not at all off limits or unavailable for you to obtain, nor do your counter-parts possess any type of incomparable qualities that license them to have chief priority over them, in comparison to you. But what is true is the fact that they have cognitively taken into custody something you have yet to. Your counter-parts have unearthed the importance of seeking out and utilizing those tools. Your continued search for "authentic" *blackness* has your perception of what it's going to take in order for you to outlive America's arrangement, a pact that has been designed specifically for *black* men who do not meet America's expectations, completely distorted. This is the primary reason why you have not, at least up to this point, been able to find the tools of survival of importance. As well brothers, your self-created worlds—worlds that define a real *black* man as a gangster, thug, hustler, savvy street shark, and macho figure—have cunningly lassoed your state of mind with debris from the "hood", and you must immediately decipher a system to mentally liberate yourselves in order to function resourcefully outside of your metropolitan citadels. At this moment, your state of affairs within your respected environments are parallel to a young *black* child who has entered a short distance foot race; however, because of bias revisions to event policies, they must relinquish a head start to their counter-parts in order to compete. This basically means that each individual *black* male challenger living within America's poverty-stricken localities cognitive endurance and initial steps out of the starting block must uniformly labor in a manner that quickly closes the distance between them and their opponents. As well, the form they employ must be one which is thrice as skilled as all of their adversaries and used in an even more calculated manner in order to increase their chances of winning.

Author and journalist Touré, in his recently written book *Who's Afraid of Post-Blackness?*, examined and highlighted this very objective via comedian Chris Rock's standup act *Kill the Messenger*. Through a painstakingly sad but true joke, Rock made a robust point when he spoke on the topic of there being only four *black* homeowners who reside within his predominately white multimillion dollar New Jersey neighborhood. Touré wrote, "His neighbors include Mary J. Blige, Patrick Ewing, and Eddie Murphy. Rock says Blige, Ewing, Murphy, and he are (or were) among the best in the world at their professions. Then he says his next-door neighbor is a white dentist." Touré continued, "Rock spells out the point with a devastating punchline: "The *Black* man gotta fly to get something the white man can walk to." Rock's message detailed something that we are all aware of, which is, *blacks* have the liberty of transitioning into America's upper echelons of social and living statuses, but they must not only be willing to dual with her through quadruple overtime, they must, ultimately, win in order to get there. This principle highlights the fact that white supremacy and the ideology of colonization in America are far from being a defunct movement.

It's vital that you brothers know how to compete in this biased society for the sake of being a provider, a real man, a father. I want all *black* men to understand this important fact. Your children are more likely to mimic your actions as they transition through school and on to adulthood, because they look up to you whether you believe it or not; therefore, you have to set an example that authenticates that it is alright to work hard in order to provide for your family, because the "hood" is relaying to children that the act of working is obsolete and those who work are weak. In the book I mentioned previously, *The Envy of the World,* author Ellis Cose issued *black* parents what he called rules of survival to assist them in the battle against their competition. Rule number two stated, "If you have a child or even a younger brother, odds are your choices will influence theirs; so even if you're quite willing to risk your own future, or don't think you will live long anyway, or believe there is nothing better for you in this world, are you willing to condemn those whom you should care about to share your fate?" In retrospect, Mr. James Baldwin once said, "Children have never been good at listening to their elders, but they've never failed to imitate them."

Once they become adults, children will always respect and remember how hard their mothers and fathers worked to provide for them and will likely be highly motivated to follow that admirable path. As well, I firmly believe that hard working parents are the vital asset that will help resurrect the extinction of the *black* two-parent family home, which is extremely beneficial in the task of escaping poverty as well. The monetary umbilical cord which links low-income *blacks* to the government must be cut, because this is an obstacle in which the government shaped to decelerate the progress of *blacks* within low-income communities. Those who have not proven that they have some type of physical or mental disability that enables them to work and are pupils of high risk poverty-stricken areas need to be held accountable for making provisions to sustain their own livelihood, especially for necessities such as food, shelter, utilities, clothes and transportation. Collecting on what you are considering to be wages to assist you has turned more into your monthly lottery supplement. Because of this, dependency upon the government must cease now. Wouldn't it be a lot easier to detoxify your current method of thinking and contribute to your own well being by relying on income with stability to make ends meet? Surely, doing so will sanction you to set yourself free from governmental bondage. Brothers and sisters, you have to start thinking more highly of yourselves.

But in order to carry this through, you must become financially independent. I repeat, to all of my brothers and sisters who make up low-income populations, **IT'S OK FOR YOU TO WORK!** You do not have to participate in illegal activities to earn a salary and more importantly, all of you, brothers and sisters, have some type of talent that could help you earn a lucrative income. Explore finding your talent(s), even if it means enrolling into a training class of some sort that will allow you to develop your skill sets to become certified in that particular area.

"And unto one he gave five talents, to
another two, and to another one; to every
man according to his several ability; and
straightway took his journey."
Matthew 25:15

There are more than a few trades and certifications that can provide outlets of financial freedom, as well as programs that will help you finance them. Put your pride aside, develop an independent energy, and take advantage of the temp services and job markets within your area that are possibly a good fit you. Liberate yourselves away from invalid beliefs, dependencies, and crippled practices that have outlived their usefulness and start thinking rational. *Black* people, we have to terminate this ***GHETTO MENTALITY***, and we have to do it ***RIGHT NOW***!

QUIZ 11

- **What are possible reasons that would make a father neglect his child or children? Are the elements that play a part in a parent neglecting their child legitimate reasons for them to just call it quits? Answer with precision.**

  _____

  _____

  _____

  _____

- **Do you believe that a child will ever be able to genuinely discard the negative feelings that have been implanted, due to the abandonment of their father, before they reach adulthood? Answer with precision.**

  _____

  _____

  _____

  _____

- **Why is maintaining a "Ghetto Mentality" dangerous? Do you believe this method of thinking** is a surefire way to keep one oppressed and in a mental state of immobility? Answer with precision.

_____

_____

_____

_____

- If a young child witnesses their mother or father working hard as they are growing up, will they respect them even more as parents and will that be an incentive for them to become productive citizens? Answer with precision.

_____

_____

_____

_____

- How important is it for a *black* man with kids to develop himself into a leader and model a leadership role? Answer with precision.

_____

_____

_____

_____

12

REMOVE THE BLINDFOLD

A foremost self-inflicted wound, one that is perpetually deteriorating opportunities which will assist a large number of *blacks* in the task of surviving America, at present, is the fact that they are positioning stern limitations upon themselves as well as their proficiencies while, simultaneously, daring those who reside beyond their personal worlds to tell them they are exceedingly wrong for doing so. These same individuals have bathed in the residue of self-doubt for such a protracted length of time that they have become conscientiously conditioned to only trust methods of cognitive functioning which are produced and available, exclusively, within the diminutive radius of their mangy self-constructed worlds coordinated by "hood" policies. The chief quandary with this method of thinking, obviously, is the fact that the primary manias in which *blacks* are sadistically clinging to are all of the unconstructive typecasts that mirror the "hood's" definition of "authentic" *blackness*. These unconstructive stereotypes, especially when exercised by *blacks*, just so happen to be exactly what the white dominated media pool considers essential substantiation needed to continuously remind white America that there is indeed, still, a two-class system. As a result of ingesting the media's expectations, society's version of the apple in the Garden of Eden, and continually demonstrating each, with their own hands, *blacks* have been obliviously tying blindfolds around their own eyes for decades now, trying to tread on uncharted territory. But these blindfolds must immediately be removed and by removed I mean we must discontinue living out and applying the same unconstructive stereotypes in opposition to one another that society and predominately white media pools aim at us, so that we can safely navigate our way through the smog of our debris filled paths in search of prosperity.

It escapes me that the day to day struggles and concerns of *blacks* within low-income environments are not seen as valuable distresses to media pools; instead, all of the violent consequences manufactured as a direct result of those struggles are the events which become news worthy. Media images are continuously condemning *blacks*, as they present us in a negative light via T.V., movies, literature, and daily news. Fifty percent of *black* people, ages 35-50, agree.

The media in America has, as well, assisted severely in the division of *blacks* who belong to the low-income working class and those who fall into the middle class bracket. What I found to be interesting, in relation to *blacks* being purposely stereotyped in a disapproving manner by a white dominated media pool, was what a poll performed by Pew Research Center revealed. It uncovered information proving that many low-income *blacks* felt they no longer viewed their race as one consolidated unit. This was, chiefly, because they felt education, work ethic, and, ultimately, the image the media apathetically portrayed of them created a class divide amongst all *blacks*.

Nearly 40 percent of the participants in the poll felt as though they had nothing in common with middle class *blacks,* even though the search for "authentic" *blackness* and avenue ethics do indeed extend well beyond the "hood". Surely there are a vast number of middle class *blacks* who periodically detach themselves away from the exalted values which provided them a clean getaway from the "hood", primarily, because they have found that it is actually quite complicated to completely escape, being that "hood" ethics are so robustly endorsed via the media and big screen, in addition to the fact that the values they have obtained in route to middle class living are all declined and disdained as being "unauthentic" *blackness.* The media has also planted in the minds of many, delicately, that there may just be a very strong probability that *blacks* are just not predestined to survive America by means of archetypal arrangements of accomplishments.

Albeit, an overwhelming dose of *black* actors animating incriminating roles on the big screen and T.V. programs, as well as the mass media's uncompromising focus on crime, drug use, gang violence, and other forms of insubordinate behaviors among heavily *black* populated localities, primarily low-income districts, have resulted in middle class *blacks'* perceptions of this group being tremendously fostered and skewed as they, sturdily, try to come to terms with the new acuity of low-income *blacks* in America.

As many other tactics used to protract white dominated colonization, T.V. and the mass media have played key roles in whites continuously being able to attempt to annex and own America. Even if it is unwillingly, you must admit that thus far the media has done a very sound job of earnestly planting in the mind of the masses that young *black* men and women, chiefly *black* men between the ages of 18 and 30, are nothing short of gangsters, jesters, dope pushers, floozies, and hard core murderers. These potent images which are being painted for society's viewing pleasure are all damaging short and long-term inflictions for *blacks*, because this type of treatment destroys any chances of financial advancement in terms of one acquiring a loan, promotion, or even finding a job. Illuminating and recurring negative images of *blacks* surely plant a bad taste in America's mouth, particularly for convicted felons who are being released from prison and genuinely want to redirect their lives in a positive direction. Bell Hooks, in her book *Killing Rage*, spoke to this imbalance. In reference to whites, today, colonizing America and controlling *blacks* via the new neo-colonial, T.V. and mass media, Hooks internalized racism present in education, the work force, movies, and mass media when she wrote:

> **Placed in positions of authority in educational structures and on the job, white people could oversee and eradicate organized resistance. The new-colonial environment gave white folks even greater access and control over the African American mind. Integrated educational structure were the locations where whites could best colonize the minds and imaginations of *black* folks. Television and mass media were the other great neo-colonial weapons.**

In the following two photos which were posted on *Yahoo News* during the brink of Hurricane Katrina's chaotic events, evidence that racial bias was again able to navigate its way into the mainstream media and perpetuate the effects of historical oppression is highlighted. This came during a time when those who were being gravely affected

by everything going on around them were forced to survive by any means necessary. As you view the images, pay close attention to the caption in both pictures and notice how the *black* male is accused of ***looting***, while the white couple is noted as ***finding*** groceries. What's just as appalling as the timing in which this chauvinism was executed by the media was the fact that the editors who approved and published these captions never found it important to modify the header referencing the young *black* man.

This is clearly one microscopic example of how the media fosters and distorts the image of *blacks*. In making that point, I would like to ask two substantial questions. Is it safe to imply that the media, in satisfying the needs of their elite white audiences through inadequate news coverage of *blacks*, is a modern day instrument used to continue racism (the slash) and all of its negative effects? Also, are the images of *blacks* severely tainted in the media with the premise of fraudulently positioning them to remain economically paralyzed—forbidding them to find stable employment while the white elites pile up their financial investments?

In addition to living out negative stereotypes, we (*blacks*) are decisively clinging to a pernicious idea of what an "authentic" *black* person should look, talk, and act like. This falsified image which has us hoodwinked is the same representation that the media fervently displays on T.V. and in a large number of movies for our viewing pleasure. One who exploits the overuse of the (N) word, has limited or no education, uses unheard of vernacular, women bathed in tight clothing to gain attention, and a *black* man wearing his pants down beneath his butt are the character traits that brothers and sisters living within their self-created worlds all embrace as an "authentic" African American. Anyone who does not fit this description is unquestionably rejected within the "hood" and observed as an alien to the population. This type of internal racial division creates room for another very important question. Are the values of middle class and low-income *blacks* the same? You're right, absolutely not. This is bizarre, because middle class *blacks* and middle class white's values have merged to where they are beginning to align directly with one another.

The current state that a large number of *blacks* are in, living check to check, relying heavily on the government for assistance, and indulging in all of the issues paucity offers, have gravely distorted their hopes of ever surviving America and clandestinely created a fortified alliance amongst the low-income population—an association which is well-built. What is heartrending is the fact that these brothers and sisters have whole heartedly accepted, at least cognitively, that they will never be affiliated with any type of success, whether it be didactic, financial, or personal, because all of their lives, a vast majority of them have been told that they cannot and will not amount to anything, via their peers, teachers, society, and even their own parents and guardians. As well, this immense bulk of *black* men and women, who are all influenced heavily by the "hood" and its politics, have actually accepted every negative and falsified prophesy placed upon them by America. Receiving only negative reinforcement growing up as a child, as adults, they have been cognitively conditioned to accept the limitations that man has placed upon their lives. One major problem here is that once they ultimately convince themselves that they will never amount to anything, they abandon one of the most tangible vehicles highly reliable in assisting them to, at least, obtain some degree of prosperity. That vehicle is education.

For those who quit school, most were performing at subpar levels when they were attending. Even then, their self-esteem and confidence in themselves as individuals and students were low. Attending low level classes and being the subject of ridicule, in addition to their teachers not being able to effectively teach to their deficiencies, deteriorated their confidence and compelled them to conform to a negative outlook on school. This mishap unconstructively habituated their minds as they transitioned to adulthood and outfitted them to only be able to relate to what they see in their communities: unsuccessful people, hard times, drugs, physical and verbal abuse, and murder. Although these affairs are awful, they embrace them with love, primarily, because these are the only commodities they can candidly relate to.

Case after case has proven that an aberrant paradox which continually presents itself as typical to the masses of *blacks* who remain subdued by the debris of their "hoods" is the fact that all of the horrid ingredients to a disastrous life are what make them feel accepted and successful. As odd as it may sound, through harmful actions and negative media stereotyping, a large number of *black* men and women in the "hood" feel that they succeed, at least according to the rules and regulations of their environment. Whether it's killing, stealing, robbing or becoming a victim of drug abuse, young and old, this is where they unearth personal success. Inside their homes, no one is motivated, so there is no urgency to be productive. Everything they do, say, eat, wear, and learn revolves around their environment. To them, nothing else exists beyond the city limitations that embrace their designated conurbations.

I'm reminded of a time in which I experienced this method of thinking first hand. When I was working on my undergraduate degree, I remember inviting some very close friends of mine, during that particular time, from home to come down and hang out with me my freshmen year. The entire school year, these guys never made it on campus and always hid behind excuses for not wanting to leave out of their comfort zones. Again, during my sophomore year, I invited these same friends back, this time to watch me play ball, and again they distributed multiple excuses that supposedly hindered them from visiting. By this time, without any reservations, I knew that these particular friends deemed they did not have any type of connection with the environment of a college campus, an environment that I had the privilege of penetrating with the intentions of shedding off "hood" policies, an environment whose rules and regulations contradicted everything they were conditioned to. I also became aware of the fact that they believed they would not be able to relate to any of my new friends. Even though they never admitted there was an uneasiness present, I took it upon myself to make them feel at ease by the assuring them that no one there, at least who I met or knew, acted stuck-up and by also making reference to the masses of beautiful women who were on campus.

As I progressed through school, on different occasions, I would ask these brothers if they ever thought about travelling, cognitively and physically, to additional localities and imagined themselves one day just moving away to make a life somewhere else. Each time I asked, the feedback I received was always the same. One friend in particular would always say, "I never really think about going anywhere else." To me, this not only meant that he was going to physically remain in the same locality for the rest of his life, but also in the same cognitive locality as well. Deep down, I always knew these brothers wanted to visit me, but the cognitive limitations in which they confined themselves to and the fear of being in violation of the "hood's" code of travel policy permitted them from exploring more than our neighborhoods and eventually weakened our friendship. Needless to say, these brothers never came down to visit me the entire time I was in college. Not only were my friends afraid to physically leave their comfort zones, they were also cognitively afraid as well.

QUIZ 12

- **Do you believe that overwhelming and inadequate reports of *blacks* in the news by white dominated media have actually caused a severe division between *blacks* who live middle class lifestyles and *blacks* who live in the "hood"? Explain your answer in detail.**

  _____

  _____

  _____

  _____

- **In your opinion, what are major factors that have placed barriers between *blacks* within low-income environments and *blacks* within the middle class? For example, do you believe it is salary, morals, or envy? Explain in detail.**

_____
_____
_____
_____

• What is your definition of the term "comfort zone"? Answer with precision.

_____
_____
_____
_____

• How is it possible for *blacks* to weaken the impact of stereotypes applied to them by America if they endlessly accept and reinforce them? Answer with precision.

_____
_____
_____
_____

• What are some possible solutions that will assist *blacks* in removing the blindfold that is so tightly tied and impairing their vision? Be very specific when answering.

_____
_____
_____
_____

13

BELONGING TO RELATIONSHIPS

As a child growing up, I vividly remember wedding ceremonies being so aberrant, so unexpected, that they were approached as if they were going to be nationally televised. This was primarily due to the fact that this was one event that very seldom occurred within my family or even the families of a great deal of my childhood friends. As well, because I had no one to closely observe and actually model this degree of relationship, I was unconscious of the fact that when *blacks* married, they constructed one of the most vital and essential elements needed to strengthen and sustain the *black* family structure within the *black* low-income community. Therefore, my take at a youthful age on marriage did not involve knowledge of the extensive effort, the great deal of exertion, and all of the virtues it took to sustain one—such as honesty, integrity, patience, financial stability, understanding, and being able to effectively listen to your mate—all qualities of being a notable human being, but more importantly the catalyst needed to revivify a marriage and make sure it survives.

Of all of the weddings I have attended throughout my life, there is one in particular which has always appended in my mind that I will never forget, primarily, because it was the first wedding I actually ever participated in. My cousin Jackie tied the knot when I was five years old, and I had the self-effacing privilege of being the ring bearer. It's staggering how, to this day, I can still easily recall the events of the rehearsals we attended at the church in Washington, D.C., the camphoric smell of the sanctuary, as well as my Aunt Puddin, Jackie's mother, giving me specific instructions on when and where to stop, go, and who to look for to receive my queue to enter and leave the sanctuary. I even remember how the brown suit that I wore, along with the butterfly collared shirt and massive bowtie, fitted me. I'm confident that the memories from this nuptial are still colorful, because this was the first ritual that took place within my immediate family. Since then, I have attended and participated in multiple wedding ceremonies, predominantly weddings of either a few close friends from college or distant relatives who I haven't had the pleasure of actually speaking to since childhood. Intermittingly, within my family, a wedding is an event that brings everyone together for a short duration of time, but for every wedding that takes place, it seems as if ten years passes by before there is another one.

Around the age of ten is when I truly began to come to terms with my family's ideology of the idea of marriage, primarily because all of my older cousins, aunts, uncles, and distant family members were extending our family, but no weddings were befalling. What was even more interesting was the fact that they all were in esteemed relationships, well at least that's what I perceived them to be, but no one wore rings on their fingers. At this particular age, maybe because I was at a stage in my life where I was beginning to be able to sort out the very attractive ten and eleven year old girls at school from the not so attractive ones and cordially communicate with them, I felt as if I had at least a fraction of understanding of the substructures of a sound relationship, even though the relationships within my personal environment contradicted those of my middle class white teachers.

Nearly all of my white teachers, during my years of attending middle school, would in some form or fashion relay to the *black* students from the "hood", in an indirect manner, that their household's marital statuses contrasted those of our parents. Now that I'm older, I truly don't believe this was done out of spite or with the intentions of trying to hurt our feelings, bragging, or boasting, or with the intentions of saying, "We have family structure and unity within our households and you all don't." Actually, as I reflect on each occurrence, I believe that they simply merged their personal worlds that didn't involve their commitment to us, with us. In particular, I vividly remember one of my 6th grade teachers always making mention of her husband and kids and how they endlessly participated in activities over the weekend as a unit. This was the first time that I knowingly digested a large dose of middle class living through oratory that was so vivid it made me wonder why my environment did not provide those same categories of outings for me. Mentioning that, does not witnessing multiple marriages, growing up within their immediate family, scorn or help young *black* children, especially *black* males without a father figure?

When speaking on the subject of relationships involving *black* men and women and what needs to be done in order to help bandage the lacerated wounds of not only their affairs, but their ideology of a sound relationship as well, there is a long debate regarding why *black* families are not remaining cohesive. One obvious crisis that is crippling the *black* community and perpetually weighing heavy on *blacks'* relationships, which can no longer be ignored, is one that has been highlighted by the Justice Department's figures for 2006 which revealed that 1 in 9 *black* men between the ages of 20 and 34 is currently behind bars. For *black* women who are the same age, the quote is about 1 in 150. So then, for obvious justifications, *black* male convicts today have found themselves excluded from the province of the dating pool. This is chiefly, because *black* women are beginning to steer clear of ex-cons, which makes a capacious difference when 1 young *black* man in 3 can expect to be locked up at some point early in their lives.

Some believe that the select few of *black* men who have eluded the mass imprisonment movement—a movement purposely disguised as a routine way of life by America—are neglecting their responsibilities as fathers and refuse to do the right thing while others believe that *black* women are too difficult to get along with, which is playing an equally problematic role in the breakdown of relationships, because this makes it difficult for *black* men to frequently remain in the lives of their children. In reference to this subject, I have no problem admitting that I'm no relationship guru, and I surely do not have the panacea to this quandary, nor am I trying to use this manuscript as a vehicle to reallocate you to a fictitious utopia that suggest you run off and get married immediately after reading it. But what I do know is that, in reference to *blacks* travelling on their respective paths with the goal of someday obtaining prosperity in mind, it is vital that we, while on our paths, establish and maintain quality, sound, and healthy relationships along the way. How will you ever be able to come remotely close to establishing and maintaining the needed and vigorous relationships with people who will genuinely help you handle the debris that are certain to come as a result of reaching prosperity and becoming successful, such as extensive envy from family and friends, consistent soliciting of money from cormorants, and the multitude of close family and friends who actually are going to want you to fail, if you can't establish and maintain a personal and healthy relationship within your own home—prior to penetrating the corridors of success? Again, don't misconstrue my message hear as if I am suggesting that we (*blacks*) need to only focus on strengthening intimate and marital disparities within our communities only. Although those are relationships that are vital and needed in order for the *black* two-parent home to be reborn, we also must begin valuing relationships that are business and socially oriented, formal, and informal, because you never know who is going to be able to help you miles down your road to a better life.

The existing state in which *blacks'* relationships are in is the consistent topic of conversation within the African American community. We see scores of *blacks*, whether it be relatives, friends, or colleagues, choosing to get together, but eventually they end up dissociating. One primary issue with this event, obviously, is the fact that a large number of *black* children become victims of this calamity. Mentioning this, I'm sure that you too agree that children should not be wagers in adult affairs. Still, at an alarming rate, they are suffering drastically, because once their parents disconnect, they no longer see their mothers and fathers as parental sentries; instead, they view them as baby mamas and baby daddies, who from their peers and family members the same age as them, are already aware of the lifestyle that comes along with one parent being absent from the household. What is even more depressing is that the single-parent home has now become and is viewed to young *black* children as the norm or what constitutes the definition of *black* family formation.

Children, especially those who are not part of the middle class and are detached away from the values of their demographics, desperately need to witness their parents work through noble times, but also difficult times as well, because the stifling challenges that plague and await *blacks* beyond the interior of their homes—specifically those who are products of low-income environments—will need to be riddled with diligent and sound problem solving skills which can only be acquired within a stable home. Therefore, it's pivotal children witness these skills, with their own eyes, at home. More importantly, the presence of both parents will assist in breaking the cycle of the *black* single-parent home syndrome and decrease *black* children's intensified risk of living in poverty. Mary Parke, through extensive research in an annotated Couples and Marriage Research and Policy brief published in May 2003 by the *Center for Law and Social Policy*, extracted data that revealed the evils of growing up within a single-parent home for children. While researching, Ms. Parke found that Sara McLanahan and Gary Sandefur, in 1994, used verification from four national data set deposits and compared the outcomes of children growing up with both of their biological parents to children growing up with just a single parent. In reference to their study Parke wrote:

McLanahan and Sandefur found that children who did not live with both biological parents were roughly twice as likely to be poor, have a birth outside of marriage, have behavioral and psychological problems, and not graduate from high school. Other studies have reported associations between family structure and child health outcomes. For example, one study found that children living in single-parent homes were more likely to experience health problems, such as accidents, injuries, and poisonings.

As well, President Barack Obama, in his book *The Audacity of Hope: Thoughts on Reclaiming the American Dream*, reminded us that the decline in family structure is a storm which has subsided all races, but it is within the *black* community where the effects are most paralyzing. "These trends are particularly acute in the African American community, where it's fair to say that the nuclear family is on the verge of collapse." President Obama continued, "Children who live with both their biological mother and father do better."

"The family is the corner stone of our society. More than any other force it shapes the attitude, the hopes, the ambitions, and the values of the child. And when the family collapses it is the children that are usually damaged. When it happens on a massive scale the community itself is crippled. So, unless we work to strengthen the family, to create conditions under which most parents

will stay together, all the rest—schools,
playgrounds, and public assistance, and
private concern—will never be enough."
-Lyndon Baines Johnson

I am almost certain that you will agree that children from stable and committed homes will someday have strong knowledge of what it takes to make a relationship work. As well, I'm sure that you would agree that once children who come from stable homes become adults, they will never forget the impact that the stability of their parent's relationship had on their lives and possibly make them more willing to enter into committed relationships. I am a firm believer that when children's lives began to become distorted by the erratic decisions that their parents make, at that point, it is time to draw the line and look for solutions that will work to effectively mend the *black* two-parent home back together, because surely poverty is what awaits the *black* single-parent home that is not prepared to deal with America's harsh and systematic regulations.

For as long as I can remember, I have always found it intriguing that the intimate relationships of *black* men and women have somehow been conformed to an unwritten declaration that states, "We can date for ever, but getting married in a no no." Mild discussion of the (M) word within the *black* community has somehow found a way to be just as equally sensitive as extensively discussing the (N) word in public with someone white. Mentioning that, is it safe to infer that marriage is on its last leg within the *black* community? And if so, would you agree that the ideologies of marriage, for the most part, have consciously ignored the needs and circumstances of low-income *black* couples, even though they are components of a population that desperately require all of the benefits of marriage, especially the strength of the two-parent home, because as of right now, the state of their relationships are clearly on life support and need to be resuscitated immediately.

If marriage in the *black* community is on its last leg, we have to prepare ourselves to believe that the *black* family dynamic is on its last leg as well. So then, what does this say about the cornerstone of the African American family structure? According to an analysis entitled *The Decline of Marriage and Rise of New Families*, emitted in 2008, 72% of African American women who gave birth were unmarried. This analysis was conducted by the Pew Research Center on November 18, 2010. As well, within this same analysis, the Pew Research Center supplied statistical data that documented the abrupt decomposition of American's attitudes toward marriage and family for all races. It also provided a depiction of African American family values as well:

- 61% of African Americans were married in 1960 versus 22% in 2008.
- Most Americans, including African Americans, don't feel premarital sex is wrong.
- Most Americans feel marriage is no longer a prerequisite for parenthood.

This data suggested that the African American family and family structure are dying rapidly—growing faint as if they've dined on the venomous intentions that America's ghettos have to offer. But just as anyone who desires to breathe fresh air, there are some African Americans who want these numbers to be resuscitated. In reference to this particular populace, the 2008 Pew Research analysis stated the following:

- Most Americans are optimistic about marriage.
- 74% of African Americans say that single women having children is bad for society.
- 72% of people who attend church weekly believe children should be raised in a home with a mother and a father.

Black Men

In terms of belonging to relationships, I must candidly admit that a vast majority of *black* men have not, at least up until this point, taken the necessary measures that would grant them eligibility to be considered prime candidates for substantial relationships—relationships of quality. Their ineligibility, in terms of making themselves marketable within America, has stripped them of their right to self-reliantly choose marriage, family, lucrative business associates, and obtain financial leverage. Manifold misfortunes have overwhelmed *black* men in America, but their afflictions are mainly due to socio-economic and self-inflicted variables such as a significant incarceration rate, horrific educational systems that have written them off, and exceedingly high unemployment and homicide rates.

Other than the insignificant relationships within your personal worlds which include your homeboys, women whose intensions have no merit, and immediate family members whose aspirations in life mirror yours, your social circle is one that is narrow and untrained in terms of defeating all of the task that America has coursed specifically for you. *Black* men are avidly engaging in relationships with populace who are bringing out tendencies within them that are indisputably going to lead them either into a grand state of robust ineffectiveness or worse, prison or the grave.

We all, despite your personal status, need to establish relationships that will allow us to cultivate as individuals. You brothers, especially if you desire to move towards prosperity, need to begin building relationships with people who don't just claim to care for you, but truly have a vested interest in you. More importantly, it is imperative that you brothers know that the same people who have been trying to steer you away from the destructive lifestyles you are living are going to be the same and only people who will be supporting you if you are ever hit with a lengthy jail sentence. Let's just keep it real here. Within America's streets, the same individuals who you are breaking laws with glorify that lifestyle right now as your trusted allied, but guess what? When America's calloused penalties subdue you, as a result of living a lifestyle that is listless, and places you in her back pocket, only to be forgotten about, that cell will be dreadfully lonely and those same friends who influenced and proposed reckless decisions upon you, disguised as "hood" leadership, will be non-existent.

Black men, contemplate this analogy. In the game of life, which is parallel to athletics, we feel invincible. During the most intense moments of the game, it seems as if we can see the world in its entirety, the complete field, or the whole court with perfect clarity, especially with the reputation of being the featured player; but in actuality, it's the players on the side lines, the individuals we never really talk to, the guys who genuinely care about our game plans, the ones who practice but never get in the game, the bench warmers, who actually have more visibility of the game than we do. Honestly, those are the brothers who we really should be talking to at half-time, in reference to any possible modifications in our game that we maybe need to make which will increase our chances of winning. I am almost certain that a great number of your family members have played the roles of the benchwarmer, in terms of trying to provide you with sound advice during halftime regarding your current lifestyle, as well as your friends and their value in your life, but you ignored them all.

An explicit truth in life is that most of the people who are smiling in your face and greeting you with fake hugs and hand slaps can care less whether or not you evade the massive pitfalls of the "hood", go to prison, or modify your mental state of being as an initiative to move beyond what your insolvent environment has to offer. They are fine with you recurrently engaging in self-destructive behaviors that has America grimacing at you, solely because they are looking for an out themselves, but at your expense. Just recently, through personal observation and reflecting on the path that I have travelled down, I became aware of how blessed I was to have people in my life who genuinely took a resilient interest in me, Jermaine, as a person and a young man. A countless number of people offered me support. In attendance were my mother, uncles, brothers, sister, Cynthia Horton-Jones, Mrs. Nancy Rowland (r.i.p.), Mrs. Ethelyn Phillips, Ja'von Dixon, Marlela Clark-Lebeouf, Jamie Patterson, Kwame King, Kishiro Easterling, Mr. Marshall Thompson, Dr. Louise Maynor, Dr. Tom Evans, Dr. Bocktin, high school teachers, Leshay Wiley, and Jeannine and Howard Wiley; as well, North Carolina Central University's entire English department, who through discipline, shaped me into a professional, writer, and confident African American male with a purpose. All of these individuals are humbling reminders to me that my success would not have been obtained alone.

You brothers have placed yourselves behind the eight ball by trying to trade punches with propagating enigmas alone and perpetually living out the stereotypes that America has placed before you. These stereotypes have cunningly masked your vision in such a fashion that you can only see the value of life in the form of "authentic" *blackness*. What's problematic about this hallucination is the fact that "authentic" *blackness* does not possess the essential paraphernalia that you need to survive America and build tangible relationships, notably intimate relationships. As a matter of fact, all of the paraphernalia that you need in order to survive America can only be acquired by exiting your personal worlds, exiting the "hood". I would like to remind you that the following are all exempt in the "hood": steady employment, awareness of the responsibilities of marriage, and articulation and people skills. What's also problematic is the fact that "authentic" *blackness* is only of significance within your small locality. Outside of your personal worlds, America omits even standing room only for the self-created "authentic" *black* person. More notably, the apparatuses in which "authentic" *blacks* are armed with are useless beyond the fortifications of the "hood", low-income populations, and the projects. Understand that America has purposely been constructed to reject "authentic" *blackness*.

SLAVERY'S INFLUENCE ON BLACKS' RELATIONSHIPS

To make an attempt to diligently explore possible deter-minants and stimuli that are fueling the decline in *blacks'* inability to maintain healthy and stable relationships today, particularly *blacks* living within low-income populated en-vironments, it would be impossible to arrive at a solution oriented destination without, first, flirting with the possibil-ity that a primary catalyst to this issue could in fact be the malevolent effects that slavery has unendingly pressed upon the *black* race, generation after generation. It is no secret that *black* men who were bound by slavery were compelled to allow, and in some cases witness, their slave holders have their way with their wives and daughters just so they could avoid lashings and other forms of cruelties, while consistently being referred to as "boy". The relationships connecting slave holders and *black* men were nothing less than quasi-parental dominated affiliations.

Today, as a result, a number of *black* men within their relationships find it extremely inflexible to remain faithful. One attention-grabbing entity that has been developed from this horrific event is the vast propagation of clandestine extended families within *black* communities across America via sexual cravings. What's vital to keep in mind here is that the children produced from these exterior sexual encounters, statistically, seem to not be important to the *black* men who father them, or at least as important as the actual act of participating within the sexual process itself. Mentioning this, do you believe that there is by any chance, either genetically or biochemically, an imperfection, one that comprehensively intensifies fright deep within the human genetic makeup, that has been reallocated down to *black* men today from their ancestral forerunners? And as a result of this imperfection, *black* men, only when partaking in an outsized dose of sexual activity, do not feel fearful, apprehensive, insecure, devalued, or intimidated as they exist within America, but instead, powerful, in control of their destiny, akin to a protector, actually worth something, intrepid, and valiant.

Too, a vast number of *black* men display child like behaviors as they, individually, reduce everything within the relationship to them ultimately needing their mate to transition into a role that mirrors that of their biological mothers rather than an intimate companion. Ultimately, this creates problems, because *black* women are aspiring men who are, at least, to some extent socially established and self-regulating.

Uniformly devastating, *black* women had to repeatedly endure the threat and practice of sexual exploitation, and at no time was there anyone capable of policing the injustices they encountered; as well, there was no one to protect them from becoming long-term concubines of white slave holders. Furthermore, the wives of slave holders would often callously punish *black* women for the infidelities of their husbands instead of the guilty men themselves. The following are just a select number of the many demonic retributions *black* women endured in consequence of their white slave holder's forcibly engaging in sexual acts with them: being locked in smokehouses for weeks at a time, deprived of food, lashed repeatedly, immediately separated from their children, and ultimately being tied to a tree and having their unborn child cut from their stomachs. Not only was it repulsive for *black* women to have to experience this horror, it was also dreadful for *black* husbands to have to witness scores of exploitations performed in their presence and not be able to do anything about it. These men were just too powerless to protect the women they loved.

In an attempt to explore this phenomenon further, I would like for you to, first, shelve to the forefront of your thoughts and give attention to one verity, which is the fact that even though marriage was a forbidden arrangement for slaves to engage in, they still went through great lengths to marry and considered marriage with the same enormity as whites did during that time. I make mention of this point, primarily, because that theory contradicts what is actually occurring today within the *black* community. Too, slaves were not only aware of the significance of the two-parent family home, they longed to structure their families around that model and sturdily desired monogamy, even when white slave holders arranged their marriages with unfamiliar mates who were purchased solely for the purpose of breeding.

Unmistakably, the psychological effects which engulfed *blacks* during slavery were undisputed, and the results of unremittingly enduring these malicious and irrefutable effects for such a protracted time frame, over time, fashioned coached human beings who were incapable of exercising sagacity, devoid of any deep emotions once they were set free, and found it strenuous to think for themselves. Establishing that point, an appealing phenomenon, one that considerably astonishes me, in reference to the anguish that slavery apportioned *blacks*, is that there is something favorably interesting about the cognitive impairment, the biotic augmentations which eventuated in addition to the outcomes of concentrated tormenting assembled with habitual and amplified disregarding, the feelings of social agitation produced from unrelenting scrutiny, the self destructive and combative attitudes that were fashioned as a defense mechanism, the brawny disregard in which *black* women developed for white women, the feelings of childishness instilled within *black* men as a result of being continuously physiologically dominated and referred to as "boy" while at the same time never being able to exemplify their manhood, fully, due to dictatorship, and how all of these highbrow extremities hereditarily formulated a brand new entity—*black* people today.

Pointing this out, do you believe that there is a remote possibility that all of the stern traumas of slavery have somehow found their way into the lives of *blacks* today and tainted their ability to attentively deal with rapports, whether they are on a social, intimate, or professional level? If you do believe that there is possibly some merit behind this assessment, what would you suggest be a sound solution to assist in reversing this obstruction? Conversely, if as of right now you are not quite convinced, yet, that slavery has somehow—even in the most minute fashion—impacted the lives of *blacks* today, in terms of our ability to function within relationships, for immediate confirmation, simply ride through various ghettos and project housing communities within close proximity to the locality you reside in, and examine the attitudes and dispositions of the individuals who populate them. The perpetual residues of slavery are exclusively warehoused within and pose a more violent threat to *blacks* who populate destitute localities excluded from America's comfort. As a matter of fact, these locations are where the threats of slavery's deadly effects, effects that were purposely conceived as *blacks* transitioned through the Middle Passage, initially have the opportunity to agonizingly pierce the veins of *blacks* living within America today who are in search of prosperity.

Even still, this poltergeist like phenomenon is not solely limited to contemporary metropolitan plantations; it does indeed extend itself into the *black* middle class arena as well, but for the select few who are able to elude this mystical banshee's confiscation via a calculated escape route, even slightly wounded, their chances of completely recovering are much greater than those living within destitute localities. For some mysterious reason, slavery's deadly effects seem to weaken, downgrade to a category which is soon undetected on radar the further away from the plantation they travel, as if the middle class arena has some type of kryptonite like effect on them.

I don't believe that *blacks*, today, will ever come remotely close to relating to the helplessness that our enslaved forerunners must have felt as they volleyed back and forth with the weighted cognitive and physical oppression afflicted upon them by white slave holders. Excluding shame and feelings of powerlessness, can you imagine the psychological distortion in which *black* slaves conceived from an event that hauled so much revulsion? I'm comparatively certain that the protracted years of grave treatment in which our ancestors endured has genetically been dispatched into the lives of *blacks* today. As well, is it safe to assume that there is a connection between *black* slaves, men and women, who escaped into their own self-created personal worlds of severe denial only to deceive themselves into believing that what they were experiencing and going through was normal and ok, and *blacks* today who have a surplus of pride and refuse to deal with events that have altered their lives— events that have negatively affected every relationship they have been in? I will not extend my premise on the effects of the tragic crimes of slavery as the sole premise for *blacks'* relationships not functioning properly today, but I do deem that they all are active means that make the pains we have endured a continued tradition.

SOCIETIE'S INFLUENCE ON BLACKS' RELATIONSHIPS

I am fully aware of the fact that white America, too, occasionally find themselves tussling with the woes of relationship anxieties, as well as atypical matters that weigh heavy on their commitments to one another, and it's not only *blacks* who merge with these afflictions. What has seemed to have gone undetected, however, is the fact that white's relationship woes and tribulations don't possess the same amplified sting that *blacks* possess. For the most part, white couples can separate and their children will still have a more intensified chance of escaping poverty's abrasions than *black* children. As well, the decline in marriage numbers seems to visit their localities far less than that of *blacks* living amongst low-income populations. It is so obvious to see that America has made sure that her prime investments, primarily white males, have and will continue to be prepared for the quest of two-parent family life, as well as fatherhood, by investing unyieldingly in them—covertly providing them with the essential tools needed to win in America: eminent education, superiority within the work force, as well as immunity to the glass ceiling concept. While this is taking place within white oriented localities, *blacks*, in particular those living within low-income circumstances, are faced with the residue of post slavery handicaps which are the formation of ghettos, inner city woes, ineffective public school systems, and disintegration of *black* families. Not to mention *black* women are highly magnetized to the shortage of marriageable *black* men due to an imbalance in availability. This proposed imbalance is largely caused, in part, by high rates of male homicide and suicide, high rates of unemployment among low-skilled *black* men, especially young *black* men in urban areas, and high rates of *black* male incarceration.

QUIZ 13

- Do you believe that slavery is responsible for the high levels of *black* residential separation from the white world? Answer with precision.

  _____

  _____

  _____

  _____

- In your opinion, what are some post slavery obstructions responsible for the fragmenting of the *black* family today? Answer with precision.

  _____

  _____

  _____

  _____

- In terms of belonging to relationships, what would you suggest that *blacks* do in order to enhance their ability to function within relationships outside of their personal worlds?

  _____

  _____

  _____

  _____

- Is it possible that *blacks* today view marriage and all of its elements as a form of oppression? Do you believe that this is the catalyst that deters *blacks* from marriage? Answer with precision.

  _____

  _____

_____

_____

- **What are personal values that govern your lifestyle and your ability to nurture and grow successful relationships? Answer with precision.**

_____

_____

_____

_____

14

NIGGER, WHO CAN SAY IT, AND WHO CAN'T??

The (N) Word

In order to explore the word Nigger, we must first, assiduously, examine its historical path, so that a meaningful understanding of this illicit utterance will be found. Traced from the Latin word Niger, which means *black*, the word Nigger made copious transitions as it journeyed from Spain, Portugal, France, and finally into the United States. Although this one word has changed hands with many different countries, its core meaning has basically remained stable—always referencing the color *black*. Despite the derivation of the word, by the 1800's, especially within America's heavily populated slave regions, it was instituted as a deprecating term meant to describe *black* slaves during this particular time, as well as spread abhorrence against them. For the duration of slavery, the word Nigger established itself as a banshee which summoned *blacks* to tyranny order. It was no longer used solely as an illustrative representing color, but as a stiletto to verbally and physically assassinate all *blacks* and separate them from humanity.

Life itself during slavery was a gauntlet for *blacks* in which they were contested to transition through routinely. As well, during this time, the word Nigger was an additional gauntlet strapped to death, strapped to spikes of hate, strapped to spears of detest which pierced *blacks* inner most essence and spiritually cudgeled them to death. When used by whites, the word Nigger exemplified *black* barring from society and worked as an oral motive to blatantly discriminate. Despite how the word was used, whether as a noun or an adjective, it magnified the typecast of *blacks* as dirty, disgusting, insignificant, inhumane, people who were paupers, listless, lethargic, good for nothing, and as a race who had no interest in obtaining skills that were necessary for upward social mobility. To reach the masses and enlighten the white world on the hate movement, even white ministers impelled the word Nigger into their Sunday morning sermons—hoodwinking congregations in to believing that their god was white and he deemed *blacks* to be their servants eternally. This was done with one goal in mind and that was to make their congregations despise *blacks*, and it worked.

As slavery expanded throughout the South, the use of the word Nigger intensified by all whites, mainly slave masters. In order to appear as autocrats, white overseers used the word Nigger in manner so menacing that slaves themselves begin to believe that they were inhumanly strange. By presenting themselves as poltergeist, slave owners were able to mentally and physically control a vast population of defenseless *blacks* and obstruct any chances of them remotely reinventing themselves or attempting to satisfy their hunger for knowledge or freedom. Stern mental and physical oppression assured whites that *blacks* would never be able to plot escapes or revolt against them. This was the primary reason why *blacks* were denied any invitation to learn how to read, spell, become familiar with the alphabet, or calculate. As well, for that reason, the word Nigger, in addition to all of its accompanying malicious epithets, was also used to refer to *blacks* being unintelligent and uneducated.

As I highlight these obstructions, is it just me or do you, too, see a clear-cut correlation between *blacks* today and their lack of interest in becoming educated and our ancestors educational deprivation that they were forced to conform to as slaves? Would it be safe to presume that the act of declining education as a means of escaping poverty today for *blacks* is a direct result of the traumas of slavery? Is it also safe to assume that delicacies such as first-class dominion of speaking English assertively and possessing a quality job are considered to be weak and contrary to *blacks* in pursuit of "authentic" *blackness*, because these are what they consider to be attributes of the white race? I raise these questions, because it escapes me that we continually throw away the memory of our ancestors who, during slavery and after, were at times brutally eradicated for seeking knowledge. Nonetheless, they still painstakingly pursued it. It makes no sense at all for us (*blacks* today) to believe that we are racially unsuited to become educated and continually turn a blind eye to its worth.

Moreover, stemming from the word Nigger, degrading nicknames were created to assist in the dehumanization and assassination of *black* people's spirit and character, such as (coon, jiggaboo, darky buckwheat, colored and monkey). But as you can see from the diagram, the word (Nigger) is at the apex of a very extensive pyramid of racial slurs that have been aimed at *blacks*. Soon these names be-

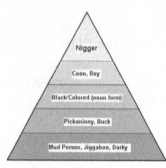

came main stream and were filtered through American society, mainly via literary works, cartoons, and motion pictures, but in addition to those outlets, they were also promoted publicly on billboards, which permitted negative stereotypes of *blacks* to take on a life of their own. Likewise, this hierarchy of malevolent appellations was purposely constructed by an initiative that justified the continuation of deception, mistreatment, and amplified terrorization to permanently immobilize *blacks* in an adolescent type state. Simultaneously, whites disfigured the image of *blacks* on a broader scale promoting prejudice along with tyranny and hate.

In 1874, The McLoughlin brothers produced and distributed a game puzzle called "Chopped Up Niggers" and in 1916 an ad from a magazine published by Morris & Bendien displayed a picture of a *black* baby drinking ink from an ink container which was labeled "Nigger Milk". These images alone will make even the most habitual user of this word, today, yield to the notion of ever allowing this epithet to take production in their mouths again.

The famous words that Mr. James Baldwin spoke, ***"You can only be destroyed by believing that you really are***

what the white world calls a Nigger," were a firm reminder to Negroes during his time that they were nothing less than human and being a Nigger started in the mind. Those words were also a subservient navigational tool to humble *blacks* as they travelled down a course of racism that was particularly designed to destroy them. In America, racial remarks have victimized all ethnic groups, but none have affected those groups and afflicted as much psychological pain in the same manner that the word Nigger has to the *black* race. This is primarily, because no other epithet in American culture or history clutches as much intentional vindictiveness as the word Nigger. A steady diet of contempt and hate kept the white race unremittingly persecuting the character and psychological state of mind of *blacks.* Incidents such as these were responsible for *blacks'* individuality and self-esteem being stripped away from them.

Today, the use of the (N) word remains a primary catalyst for one to be found guilty of exercising nothing less than racism, particularly, if used by someone beyond the peripheral of the African American race. More severely, if used recklessly, one is almost guaranteed a severe beat down. But how is this so when *blacks* label themselves, as well as each other, the (N) word all of the time? Why does the verbal use of the (N) word by *blacks* akin the same influences as the "I can talk about my momma, but you can't" axiom in reference to exterior races exercising their right to verbally flirt with the word? That's only confirmation that we (*blacks*) are not completely unacquainted with our history and the destruction this word executed throughout the duration of slavery, but instead, unequivocally unconscious of the filtrated residue that the (N) word currently smears over our existence. Still, we have somehow transformed the word "Nigger", a word that was once used to suffocate and bring death to our entire existence, into an entity we perceive to now be cool enough to verbally flaunt, but sacred enough to protect from the world. At the same time, we have vigorously convinced exterior races, chiefly whites, not to tamper with its sensitivity by highlighting the severe consequences. History has proven that the consequences stemming from the inappropriate use of the (N) word have been issued through physical disputes and courtrooms. Again, it escapes me that we have found a way to make the very last word that an incalculable number of *black* slaves heard just before they were lynched and dismantled a part of our everyday vernacular, and for entertainers, a means to generate a million dollar income.

In relation to poverty, the (N) word has done a sensible job of marrying *blacks* to the ideology that prosperity is off limits for those who wish to obtain it in a manner that contradicts "hood" policies; therefore, an implicit metropolitan dictum has been created amongst *blacks* that states, "We should forfeit our right to attempt to reach a prosperous tier of living, especially through corridors that involve adopting somewhat middle class morals and values." This phenomenon is the direct result which has been formulated from not only the immensity of the bag in which the (N) word has transported around its collar for decades, but more so the potent contents which have been housed inside of it. Every time this word is uttered, today, it's as if we are pulling out all of the lethal contents from that weighted bag which brutally plagued our ancestors in addition to the deadly psychological effects they were dealt. What's even more dangerous is the verity that the more we utter this word, the more we momentarily and subconsciously relive our forerunners' past which inactivates our cognitive mindsets, obliviously forcing us to become recoiled thinkers who are unable to move beyond counter-productivity.

I personally believe that there is a strong negative contingency attached to the (N) word which keeps us (*blacks*) cognitively immobile and ensnared within our own self-created worlds—worlds which suggest to *blacks* that they are suppose to be and remain underprivileged as well as live destructive lives. These forged worlds also somehow bully us, as we dare to exit in fear of leaving and being detached away from the identity that we have been psychologically duped into believing we must permanently merge with. This negative unforeseen *"thing"* continuously has us cheering and rooting for failure. What's so treacherous in regards to this phenomenon is that *blacks* within low-income localities are actually accepting failure, as if it is ok. A steady consumption of (the threat), or better yet our counterparts' expectations of us, has made us (*blacks*) permanently queasy. It's been long enough that we have, decade after decade, digested societies expectations of us with the idea of getting fed. The more we internalize, the more the *black* race becomes anemic.

Every suppressed group here in America has internalized and given into society's expectations at some point in time, but we (*blacks*) have taken the internalization process and tallied its negative contingencies with everything negative within our own environments. A grave result of this wicked mathematical act is the fact that we have elected not to break free of our personal worlds. Consequently, the following actions are conceived: downplaying and denying education as a tool to escape poverty, succumbing to "hood" expectations, allowing ourselves to believe gangs and crime are a replacement for genuine love and family acceptance, and placing extreme value on non-tangible materials.

We (*blacks*) have somehow been predetermined by our environments to become, if we have not yet already been conformed, what is stereotypical and expected of the (N) word and America knows this. Hand slapping, slick vernacular using, crime seeking *black* men in sagging pants, money hungry *black* women in tight clothes, non-readers, and small minded and limited thinkers are the characters in which the "hood" seems to be promoting and producing; therefore, America is cashing in on this manufacturing process by placing these exact prototypes on the big screen. As a result, millions are made annually from these forged images of *blacks*.

But what we (*blacks*) do not see on the big screen are the round table discussions which take place between movie producers and film companies prior to making these types of movies. Amongst themselves, the topic of discussion by participants at these round table assemblies is how *blacks* who are conforming to all of the stereotypes associated with the (N) word are so beyond redemption that they deserve any outcome the "hood" offers them. Here again is where we (*blacks*) are suckered by America into believing that an "authentic" *black* does indeed exist and in order to become this "authentic *black*" we must yield to the (N) word and all that it entails.

Let me make myself unmistakably clear here. I am not suggesting that blame be placed on white America for the actions of *blacks* that have been self-damaging. What I do believe to be true, though, is that through a white dominated media pool, America is circuitously advancing to *blacks*, especially those with no desire to obtain prosperity, that it is ok for them to continuously drape themselves in all of the contingencies that the (N) word has to offer as long as they continue to do so within their own neighborhoods and also if they (white media) can continue to profit from those actions. A valid example of this buffoonery can be found on the *BET* network station.

When crimes are committed within ghettos and low-income localities, those who reside beyond the perimeters of ghetto housing walls immediately refer to the perpetrators of the crimes as the (N) word. I remember hearing one of my former *black* female students actually finding humor in various criminal acts, in reference to various races committing crimes, as well as the difference between the word Nigger and African American. She stated to another student, "White people do dumb stuff they know they can't get away with and Niggers are always doing something that has to do with drugs and guns." You must ask yourself where did this assessment, one in which this young lady deemed in her heart to be true, develop? I'm almost certain that beyond the corridors of her personal environment, society assisted in her conceiving her assessment by presenting negative images of *blacks* to her on a platter via movies and music. As a result, in this particular case, this young ladies definition of a Nigger and an African American were both different. She viewed a Nigger as being a *black* woman and man, primarily a *black* man, who will always be involved in some type of criminal activity, has nothing of high-quality on his mind, is a threat to society and law enforcement, and ultimately a hostile individual who will surely soon find himself either in the ground or in a cell before he is twenty-five years old. Her view of an African American was a *black* person who was more in tune with the perspectives of the white world and lived a life that mirrored the characters on the 80's hit T.V. series, *The Cosby Show*.

For years *black* entertainers, chiefly rappers and comedians, have instituted numerous methods to vigorously flirt with the use of the (N) word and make their audiences forget about the fact that it once embodied demons of white supremacy, hatred, and death for all *blacks*. Most rappers, today, who use the (N) word within their music all seem to have married its meaning to a particular lifestyle which contradicts its true meaning. They use it in a manner that acknowledges the ultimate fashion of one being gangsta, cool, hip, avenue thorough, having sufficient amounts of swagger, one who show cases multiple multicolored diamond chains and watches, one who possesses large amounts of money, sleeps with multiple women, and collapses to the ideology of being an "authentic" *black* person, but very seldom do many of them use it in a manner that informs listeners of the fact that the behaviors attached to the (N) word are exactly what we (*blacks*) do not want to or should be willing to casually exemplify.

Rapper Nas, in 2008, created a multitude of controversy of his own upon releasing his ninth studio album in which its original title, *Nigger*, was changed due to all of the debates surrounding the racial epithet. This particular album is distinguished for its political content, diverse sources of productivity, and its proactive subject matter. Nas, a very lyrically and politically inclined Hip-Hop artist, through neither the content nor the title, was not implying that the use of the (N) word should continue to be used by *blacks* against one another. He was strategically highlighting the fact that he understood and was well aware of all of the nuances associated with the use of the word. In his defense against all of his critics who summoned him for wanting to use "*Nigger*" as the title of his album, Nas made a very sound and plausible statement when he said, "If Cornel West was making an album called *Nigger*, they would know he's got something intellectual to say," Nas resumed, "To think I'm gonna say something that's not intellectual is calling me a *Nigger*, and to be called a *Nigger* by Jesse Jackson and the NAACP is counter-productive, counter-revolutionary." Although I did not initially agree with the fact that Nas aspired to use a word that has found a way decade after decade to place the *black* race in a paralytic type state as the title of his album, I did agree that his argument had merit, solely, because the assessment of art lies in its ability to re-trap reality.

As for *black* comedians, they have taken the (N) word, as well as its meaning, and somehow managed to turn it into an acoustic time machine that is somewhat therapeutic, leaving us wanting to continuously hear them say the word over and over again. I found this to be true while watching comedian "Earthquake" in the standup comedy movie, *An All New Comedy Experience*, as he somehow vibrantly redefined the (N) word's mandate while hilariously paralleling *blacks* in the "hood" to terrorists. Asked by his white friend, "Aint you afraid of terrorist," he replied, "F-no, I'm a nigga. I've been living with terrorist all my life." His tone, gesture, and facial expression as he says the (N) word somehow humorously conveniences his audience that the *black* experience here in America has made him a warrior who is fearless of any confrontation the world or any would be terrorist could possibly offer him. The use of the (N) word in this case is distributed to the audience with the same means of one laughing to keep from crying. For years, dating back to Mr. Richard Pryor in his prime, comedians used the (N) word in a manner that pulled satire from its deadly meaning. *Black* and white audiences alike have been conditioned by entertainers to turn a blind eye and forget, at least momentarily, about the malicious ambition that this word was and still is designed to do to the *black* race. Because of its extreme use, one could easily assume that *black* people today are unaware of the level of hatred and abhorrence that this word still has attached to it. No other word carried, and still to this day, carries as much intentional cruelty as the word "*Nigger*" does. No matter if they are positive or negative, words express vigorous concepts and ideas. The use of the word "Nigger" perpetuates stereotypes while applying the same resilient effect to *blacks* today that our ancestors felt from it throughout slavery. As for the late great Richard Pryor, a comedian who tenaciously established his initial standup acts around the unwarranted use of the (N) word, while on a trip to Africa meant to redefine himself, soon found that the visit would affect him immensely. Pryor vowed, in a hotel lobby, upon returning to the United States, to never use the (N) word again. In his 1982 comedy classic, *Live at Sunset Strip*, Pryor exclaimed:

> One thing that happened to me that was magic was that I was in the hotel lobby and a voice said, "What do you see? Look around." And the voice said, "You see any Niggers?" I said, "No." It said, "You know why? Cause there aren't any." I'd been there three weeks and hadn't said it. And it started making me cry, man. That's a devastating word. That had nothing to do with us. We come from the first people on the earth. I left regretting ever having uttered the word on stage or off it.

It was from that point on that the (N) word became obsolete throughout the duration of Richard Pryor's standup career.

Growing up, I persistently heard the (N) word used without encumbrance by older family members in various manners that labeled and categorized their friends, family, and even white people. Depending on the situation, they would use the (N) word to speak about a person who they considered to be either rotten or no good, extremely good people, or a white person with *black* people's tendencies and habits. It wasn't until I became older that I found out that the use of the (N) word along with its inborn evils attached to it, are what continues to sting *blacks* and produces within them paralytic methods of thinking. These methods of thinking easily hoodwinks one into relinquishing their right to recognize their full potential, opting to not be productive, and more severely, envying *blacks* who have maximized their abilities. I can vividly recollect this actually happening as I grew up as well. All of the older adults, whether they were family members or friends of the family, who charged their vocabularies with the constant use of the (N) word were not lawyers, doctors, or even representatives of the middle class. These were all lower class *blacks* who felt as if *blacks* who were financially prosperous where no longer in tune with the struggle white America pressed upon them, no longer able to relate to their pains, their anguish. These resentful feelings were the catalyst which kept the (N) word constantly emerging from their mouths. This is the same vicious cycle that is being replicated today. The gap separating prosperous *blacks* from those who have allowed life to suffocate their dreams has grown increasingly wide. Those who haven't made it out of their personal worlds seem to be compelled to remind those who have that they are still the (N) word. Is doing this really suppose to remind the brothers and sisters who have worked their behinds off to escape poverty that they have sold out or are some *blacks* just extremely bitter? What I believe to be true is while on this long road to failure, a road that was specifically designed for the entire *black* race decades ago, some of us made a conscious decision to merge.

QUIZ 14

- **What is your personal definition of the word Nigger? Define with precision.**

  _____
  _____
  _____
  _____

- **Do you believe that when *blacks* use the (N) word against one another they are participating in the act of racial dehumanization? Answer with precision.**

  _____
  _____
  _____
  _____

- **Is it safe to assume that all *blacks* who deem that it's ok to use the (N) word feel this way only, because they have never been called the (N) word by someone white who had evil in their heart? Answer with precision.**

  _____

_____
_____
_____

- Do you believe that there is a direct connection between the recycling of the (N) word, a word that was specifically designed to eradicate and dehumanize *blacks* for eternity, and poverty? Answer with precision.

_____
_____
_____
_____

- In your opinion, do you believe that the word Nigger will ever relinquish its power and one day be retired from the lives of the *black* race? Answer with precision.

_____
_____
_____
_____

15

GANGSTA RAP, ITS NEGATIVE EFFECTS ON BLACKS

In a personal survey I conducted within two different housing project communities, I asked several individuals, although somewhat rhetorical, if they had physically lived or travelled anywhere else other than where they were currently existing. I also asked if they had ever mentally envisioned themselves owning their own business or thought about how life would be if they rigorously altered their existing lifestyle. Nearly all of these individuals attested they had yet to practice either; in fact, they all referred to their environment as a menacing world within a world in which all of its occupants are unmanageably restricted to. After hearing various testimonies, I hastily concluded that this is primarily why this entire population is unable to envision success. Their only encounters with tangible personal growth and distant destinations come to them through society's murky windows: television, the internet, hard edged rap music, and movies. Of the four, hard edged rap music, gangsta rap music in particular, is most influential and plays a huge role within the inner-city population.

Both, *black* men and women alike, spellbound within America's urban districts are heavily influenced by this music and depend on it, because it functions as the ghetto's own personal *CNN* network. Gangsta rap, with its heavy dose of violent overtones and sexual undertones has managed to keep its listeners, specifically *blacks* living within poverty saturated populations across the nation, affixed to one another; and in a large number of cases, it has even encouraged rebellion against authority. What I find to be extremely stupefying is that *blacks*, mainly *black* males, are depending on this genre of music to assist in the validation process of their "hood" credibility and "authentic" *blackness*. This is solely, because they feel as if gangsta rap artist can thoroughly relate to their current state of living, so they revere these artists for their attitudes of reluctance when it comes to bowing down before society. This genre of music acoustically laces each listener's ear with lyrics that consists of "hood" guidelines, rules, and regulations which must be abided by in order to maintain their healthy "hood" statuses or to be considered as a member of a privileged urban macho fraternity.

Through lyrics and music videos, gangsta rap commends personal failure and vicious gangsta conduct, such as violent behavior. One of the most lethal inflictions that this particular genre of music poses upon the *black* community is that it encourages *black* men to use, manipulate, and have sex with multiple women to earn status, but fails to mention to them how to be first-class fathers to their children. Many of these listeners, male and female, are at risk and in dire need of a father figure and positive self-motivating messages from sources that extend beyond their personal environments, messages that are contrary to what the media relinquishes.

As well, a major detriment in relation to gangsta rap music is that the primary audience that this particular genre influences is becoming so dangerously subjugated by the false reality of the gangsta rap world that they are allowing themselves to be lead down a road to destruction, both male and female. Already blindfolded to reality, down on their luck, and struggling with their day to day obstructions, this vast audience is eagerly striving to be a neighborhood success overnight. Because of this, as well as various additional personal obstructions, every last one of the topics that gangsta rap promotes is highly glorified and sought after by *black* men and women who closely follow this music. A somber reality is that the music entertainment industry is well aware of this trend and because there are so many *black* inspiring rappers, especially *black* urban men, who are willing to trade their souls for what they believe to be a huge payday and an opportunity to live a so-called gansta's lifestyle, these record labels are listless, in reference to the strength of their legitimate skills as an artist or how the music they will make will affect their primary audience. This is why we, via local Hip-Hop radio stations, are continuously being served verbal trash rap from so-called "hood" rappers on a perpetual basis. And because record labels financially support this trash, gangsta rap has been able to evade challenge, in reference to its airtime being restricted, and easily maneuver to the forefront of the scheduled daily playlist of all major radio stations across the country—remaining in steady rotation. The airtime gangsta rap is granted extends far beyond that of any genuine and quality hip-hop record.

For the sake of a dollar, record labels are signing, aiming, and shooting these untalented rappers directly at a bulls-eye of self-destruction. As a result, a major collapse for these young so-called street cadets, who in most cases are virgins to broad public exposure, is that once they have inked their souls away for the likes of a short-term record deal, they will immediately be held accountable by their "hoods" to be man enough to do what they rap about. Personally, I view these particular types of rappers as a group of bamboozled individuals who are puppets for some round table of executives attempting to convey to listeners the false definition of what a real *black* man is.

I am almost certain that there are a large number of authentic hip-hop fans out there who are aware of trash rap and verbal garbage when they hear it and have enough wisdom to ignore it. Even though, one would be extremely gullible to believe that such a perspective has no factual affect on *blacks* who glorify gangasta rap's ingredients. There are an overwhelming number of *blacks*, in terms of listening to music, who have a serious problem with consuming only the protein and extracting the skeleton. This basically means they find it extremely difficult to separate the lyrics of these songs, which are propelled by anger, sexual exploitation, violence, and crime, from reality. As a result of trying to live out a lifestyle that is painted by gansta rap lyrics and what their environments glorify, the debt that these individuals are paying in order to appear cool, according to "hood" guidelines, is equating to lengthy jail sentences and, more severely, costing them their lives. *Blacks*, more specifically young *black* men without guidance or role models in their lives, are slipping from society's grasp faster than we can catch them. But it's particularly infuriating to see white America cashing in on the carnage. In 2006, civil rights activist Rev. Al Sharpton made some very essential points in reference to gangsta rap when he spoke at the annual *National Association of Black Journalists* conference in Indianapolis. Mr. Sharpton gave an address that warned of the dangers of doing nothing about the glorification of a gangster lifestyle. In this address, he stated, "We have got to get out of this gangster mentality, acting as if gangsterism and *blackness* are synonymous." Mr. Sharpton continued, "I think we have allowed a whole generation of young people to feel that if they're focused, they're not *black* enough. If they speak well and act well, they're acting white, and there's nothing more racist than that." Regardless of how you personally feel about Rev. Al Sharpton, you have to agree with the comments he made to the *NABJ* panel in reference to *blacks* yearning to live gangsta lifestyles.

In relation to gangsta rap, the three minute video it is escorted by reinforces misdeeds and violence with horrific images, but not the consequences of those negative actions. Here, too, is where *black* men and women are being visually and psychologically misled, due to the fact that they are unaware of what really takes place on the site of these video shoots. The lifestyle glorified within gangsta rap's music videos is a dangerous proposition within urban America, mainly, because some of our young people are viewing them and then attempting to live out what they see.

I want all of the brothers and sisters within urban populations to really understand that the entire rap industry is an entertainment business, just as the *WWF* and its team of wrestlers who sell acts to the public. You must understand and be more cognitively aware of the fact that these acts are not reality. Once the director yells, "Cut," all of the expensive cars go back to the dealerships, jewelry is returned to the jewelry companies, and the beautiful models are on their way to the next video shoot. These are just a fraction of the industry clandestines in which gangster rap lyrics and videos do not reveal to its followers. Karen Hunter, in her book *Stop Being Niggardly*, weighed in on this very same concept of rap music and videos when she noted, "*BET* has done a very poor job of promoting the positive images of *black* men and women with consistent negative, violent, and sexual visual images it gives viewers annually."

I previously made mention of the fact that gangsta rap music if digested inappropriately, via videos or strident speakers, can easily persuade its intransigent listeners to engage in and exhibit deplorable behaviors, especially those who are living within their own reality. As well, Ms. Hunter found this account to be true when she wrote, "You are what you view and what you read. Your television, movie, and reading diet define you perhaps more than anything else. These images can either reinforce the deep-seated self-hatred many of us carry as a remnant of slavery, or they can break down the stereo-types and create a whole new reality." Likewise, within a 2003 journal written by John H. McWhorter entitled *How Hip-Hop Holds Blacks Back*, he furnished a personal account of an encounter he experienced while in a restaurant where *black* males, who to begin with should have been in school during that particular time, were swathed in the residue of rap music while severely undermining authority as they were throwing food at one another and ignoring the manager's request to leave until she dialed in security. McWhorter wrote:

> What struck me most, though, was how fully the boys' music-hard-edged rap, preaching bone-deep dislike of authority—provided them with a continuing soundtrack to their

antisocial behavior. So completely was rap ingrained in their consciousness that every so often, one or another of them would break into cocky, expletive-laden rap lyrics, accompanied by the angular, bellicose gestures typical of rap performance. A couple of his buddies would then join him. Rap was a running decoration in their conversation.

In contrast to negative gansta rap music, I would like to highlight that not all rappers glorify violence, promote corruption, and utilize harsh lyrics. There are rappers who use their lyrical talents to socially challenge and motivate *blacks* to mentally evolve, so that they can create possibilities to improve the current conditions they are living amongst through self-empowerment. Unfortunately, though, because their lyrics are a threat to all of the propagandas of an "authentic" *black* person and there is a great chance their music could possibly root reform in populations where gansta rap has overwhelmed its listeners, as well as the fact that it is not what record labels deem as profitable, their air time is severely minimized. With that in mind, I would like to affirm that I'm not attempting to deter any inspiring rappers from living out their dreams. The focus here is on gangsta rap music and the negative effects of it.

One could parallel the entire gangsta rap industry to a chef in a very upscale restaurant preparing the perfect meal. While in the kitchen, the chef never reveals himself, the dirty dishes he's piled up, flour dispersed all over the place, nor the food that hit the floor and was possibly placed onto your plate, anyway, after a thorough wipe down. As consumers, we only see the finished product, which is a lavish cuisine that looks as if it came from a kitchen directly out of an immaculate utopia. Even though we are blind to what's actually going on in the kitchen, we eat the food anyway. Again, the gangsta rap industry functions in the same manner. As customers, you will never see what makes the business operate or the smudged divisions of the business, such as the enormous amounts of debt rappers accumulate and stress of not selling records, only the finished product. As well, gangster rappers will never reveal in their music that once they pay numerous legal and attorney fees, they earn roughly 20 cents from each album they sell, and that's being generous. Therefore, through gangsta rap the ghetto is only aware of the issues that are happening in their neighborhoods and every ghetto around the world, because the music industry only reveals to them the finished product, which is ghetto life. Even yet, a vast audience digests the finished product without checking the validity of what they are consuming.

For the record, I'm a huge fan of the hip-hop genre, and I too understand that within the music artist are merely painting a picture of what has actually materialized around them or what may be going on within their personal environments, but portraying drug lords, degrading women, and promoting violence are abominable and counter-productive to the entire African American culture, in terms of encouraging its most attentive listeners to transition away from their poverty-stricken living conditions.

QUIZ 15

- **In your opinion, is there a significant difference between rap and hip-hop music? Descriptively elaborate.**

_____

_____

_____

_____

- If it is not digested properly, meaning the visual facade that gangsta rap music and its videos exude, how dangerous can rap be to someone who is living within their own self-created reality? Answer with precision.

_____

_____

_____

_____

- Do you feel as though the hip-hop industry is exploiting the lifestyle of many poor urban *blacks* as well as inspiring new illicit activities in the name of profit? Answer with precision.

_____

_____

_____

_____

- Because gangsta rap's most loyal audience is mainly poverty-stricken *black* males and females who are living in their own realities, do you think that there is any type of indirect or direct correlation between this genre of rap and metropolitan homicide rates that are crushing *black* communities across America when you examine variables such as: poverty, unemployment, lack of education and demographics? Answer with precision.

_____
_____
_____
_____

- **In your opinion, is genuine hip-hop music more than just words and beats? Answer with precision.**

_____
_____
_____
_____

16

PERSONAL SUCCESS

It's been long enough that *blacks* have dieted on massive quantities of tainted ghetto polices-policies that have severely poisoned and coerced *black* communities across the country into an anemic state, in terms of overall merit, allure, and personal escalation. These same policies have obliged *blacks* to conceive and labor under ideologies pertaining to *black* victimization as well as *black* anti-intelligentsia—two primary self-subjugating characteristics of "authentic" *blackness.* Too, ghetto policies, along with all of the negative stereotypes in which *blacks* continue to live out, have positioned themselves so securely within their cognitive frameworks that a large number have totally failed to remember that it is critical they become success-ful in order to survive America's resilient obstacle courses which have been custom calculated specifically for them. Mentioning this, here is where we are able to see why it is so important to not exert positive energy on what has been blatantly placed before us and is unable to be altered—the fact that the plantation blue print for *blacks* in America still exist—but instead become intuitive and redirect that energy in a manner that will incite mental liberation away from all of the self-sedating characteristics of "authentic" *blackness*. Doing so will immediately permit brothers and sisters to begin envisioning success.

Success first begins in the mind; here is another quarter where we continue to fall short. *Blacks* in America who have yet to break away from the constraints of their self-created perceptions of an "authentic" *black* person have become mentally conditioned to reject pursuing paths to prosperity that will require them to use their minds. In order for you to become productive in your quest for prosperity, you will have to earnestly decide that you are going to be that only functioning light bulb that is amongst all of the broken bulbs around you.

In reference to personal growth, a culture of shared un-derstandings has been created amongst *blacks* in America. Depending on which side of the barricade you reside on, the barricade in which America has purposely constructed to deny entry to "authentic" *blackness*, you have succumb to at least one component of the segregated shared under-standings in reference to which paths *blacks* can and cannot explore in order to obtain prosperity. Let's explore this phenomenon further. A *black* person who has been college educated and values speaking correct vernacular is viewed as an abnormal *black* to those who are living amongst low-income populations, as well as those who have cognitively surrendered to the residue in which ghetto life has to offer. For this reason, the shared understandings in which *blacks* within low-income environments share are all understand-ings that revolve around the "hood" and all of its policies. Alternatively, the shared understandings in which *blacks* apportion, primarily those who cognitively live beyond the barriers of ghetto life and have distanced themselves away from the "hood" and all of its policies, mirror not only the shared understandings of those who have penetrated the middle class arena, but of all individuals, regardless of their financial strength and educational accomplishments, who have come to terms with the validity of what it takes in order for *blacks* to survive in America. Basically, *blacks* who have been informally or formally educated have acquired the necessary proficiencies which will sanction them to play both sides of the divide wall constructed by white America—increasing their chances of survival generously. What you must know is that this wall, in addition to proscribing "authentic" *blackness*, was primarily and purposely constructed to barricade all *blacks* without the necessary credentials an all access pass to America's quality jobs, profound educational institutions, and financial depositories that would allow them to create any type monetary leverage for themselves.

"Hood" policies are only valuable tools of survival for *blacks* dwelling within low-income environments. Beyond those boundaries, those policies have all proven to be useless; what escapes me is that although aware this fact, there are a vast number of *blacks* who continue to psychologically marry themselves to these hoodwinking policies that not only suppress them gravely, but also their children. As a result, these brothers and sisters are, all, failing to distinguish the validity in escaping an impoverished lifestyle. Is it remotely possible for someone to become so accustomed to living in paucity that they are soon immune to that lifestyle's shortcomings and feel as if it's normal? Let's face it, everyone does not have a million dollar athletic talent nor will they encounter the fate of mega lottery winnings. Even though, God has given each of us some unique ability that just needs to be explored and tapped into. Do you see yourself being successful? If so, you must understand that when seeking success, rigorous sacrifices must be made, which means you will have to unleash all of your aged customs and methods of operating. To begin with, the crowd or individuals you run with, the way you spend and manage your time and finances, your vernacular, and your current thought process will all have to be abandoned in order for you to be able to reinvent your entire make up. There are no exceptions to these sacrifices! These actions must be immediately exercised and carried out in order for you to even come remotely close to reinventing yourself. Only after making those strict modifications will you begin to mentally envision your plans and goals.

One pervasive and perpetual setback plaguing *black* communities today is the fact that the individuals living within them have found it reliably unimportant to align themselves with any degree of cognitive empowering, and as a result, they have dissociated themselves apart from mental labor. In fact, this populace has purposely opted to sidestep the use of cognitive muscle as a means of succeeding and potentially leveling an uneven playing field America has arranged. Some suppose that this overpowering impediment, this comatose and self-sedated method of existing, is not solely the fault of *blacks* today due to the assumption that this type of cognitive functioning is possibly the biotic residue which remains as the result of a deficient trait which has been transitioned down, genetically, from our ancestral forerunners, *black* slaves, who were not allowed to remotely explore their mental vigor. Albeit, I strongly believe that we are fully to blame today, especially with the wide spectrum of opportunities that await us, if we opt to fall victim to the enchantment of counter-productivity and choose not to become cognitively heighten in a manner which will make provisions for one to become successful. There are numerous *black* teachers, judges, police officers, and entre-preneurs, young and old, who have established themselves as living examples of what *black* success really is.

One major reproaching truth about *blacks* is that we, rather than listening with the assumption of humbling ourselves and gaining extensive knowledge from someone who has been where we are trying to go, choose not to listen at all. While placing pride on a pedestal, we disregard the abundant wisdom successful forerunners offer and fail to realize that personal success is effectively achieved in increments:

- **1st—Seek spiritual guidance through a Bible based church and a mentor. It is imperative that we seek God's strength daily and understand that anything less exploits a weakness in faith, and we become an easy mark for failure.**
- **2nd—Create your plan of action with possible setbacks incorporated within it, as well as solutions for those setbacks.**
- **3rd—Strive for self improvement and further your education.**
- **4th—Make a solid effort to separate yourself away from individuals who are dead weight and break free from public assistance.**

If you follow these four critical steps diligently, I believe you will begin to see growth promptly and windows of opportunity will begin to reveal themselves that were sealed tight before. All are imperative and positive steps that must be carried out in order for you to achieve mental and physical exodus away from the ghetto. My message to all *blacks* who desire to survive America, despite your social or financial status, is to simply reprogram your technique of thinking, detoxify your self-defeated attitudes, and commit to thinking outside of the "hood". Up until this point in your lives, you all have done things your way, and your way has not allowed you to become a valuable asset to society; therefore, switch your strategy in a manner that will at least allow you to keep one foot in the path of any closing doors.

SEEK GOD'S STRENGTH

Most importantly of all, accepting God or your higher power of choice as your savior and spiritually coloring yourself is vital not only for the sake of physically being present in a church or an equivalent sanctuary; instead, this step is solely about you submitting to God, so that you can discernibly hear from Him and be released from embedded strongholds that have held you captive your entire life. Worldly captivity has compelled you to disregard exercising faith. At this point in your life, you have developed a self-defeated attitude and lost confidence in your abilities primarily, because you have failed to exercise the faith that is needed to please God. What is faith? The Bible tells us, **"Faith is the substance of things hoped for, the evidence of things unseen," (Hebrews 11:1).**

Today, because of our broken spirits and society steered minds and hearts, we are reluctant, at times, when it comes to diligently exercising our faith unless the resources being acquired are presented directly in our faces and we can physically touch them. As much as we say we love God, do we really have faith in Him? Do we truly believe that He is the author of abundance and heavenly prosperity and that He made a solemn promise that He will never forsake us, but fulfill all of our needs if we would only trust Him? Has our walk from slavery through America's treacherous corridors broken our spirits to the point that we do not believe that there is any spiritual hope for our race? I must admit, at times it does become a challenge to exercise the diligent faith needed in reference to transitioning to prosperity, but during those most difficult moments is when you must draw even closer to God. Without faith, the journey from *Poverty to Prosperity* will never materialize, because your selfish desires will continue to inspire your plans, and your self-structured plans for your life will not manifest in the presence of God. There is a very solid chance that you're not successful right now, because

- You denounced that you could do all things through Christ Jesus who strengthens you.
- Your plan outweighs God's plan.
- You have a plan to exalt yourself, but God's plan is to bring you before great men.
- Your finances dictate whether you trust God or not.
- You fail to realize that God breaks limitations that man places upon you.
- You placed your faith in man and not God.

When you sit in a chair for the first time, do you inspect it thoroughly before sitting in it, or do you, without even thinking about it, just sit down? I am sure that you, as well as many others, have sat in a vast number of unfamiliar chairs for the first time throughout your lifetime, even in some of the most foreign places, without questioning their ability to withhold you or without giving them any type of thorough inspection, although you knew nothing about the character of those chairs. So then, how is it that we have abundant faith in something as fragile as a chair that we know nothing about, but only a fraction of that faith in God?

In reference to faith, Mario Sepúlveda Espinace, the second of the thirty trapped miners to be rescued from the chasm nearly five miles beneath the earth's surface after being pinned down for sixty-nine days in a San Jose mine, relied heavily upon his faith to get him through the three month underground ordeal that could have easily cost all of the minors their lives. In a 2010 brief post rescue interview with *CNN* Sepulveda replied, "I was with God, and I was with the devil. They fought, and God won," Sepulveda continued, "I grabbed God's hand and never doubted that I would be rescued."

> *"And God is able to make all grace abound*
> *toward you; that ye, always having all*
> *sufficiency in all things, may abound to every*
> *good work." II Corinthians 9:8*

I believe that one of the primary reasons many lack faith is the fact that they just cannot, readily, go to a shopping precinct of choice and purchase it. Mentioning that, do you believe that there is air on earth even though you can't see it? At any point throughout your day, do you decide to just stop attempting to breathe, solely because you need visual confirmation that oxygen molecules are indeed present? The enemy attempts to work against us all through our minds and hearts, so it is important that you guard them both as well as understand that if both of those chambers lack the necessary faith needed to establish a sound vertical connection with God, then you are leaving yourself exposed and vulnerable to the enemy and all of his tactics. When we sincerely renew our hearts with God and allow Him to restructure our method of thinking, our entire perspective of ourselves, our well being, and others changes instantaneously. Taking the initiative to become productive and discovering self-motivation will no longer be a dreaded task, or something that seems so hard to obtain. Everything you need will come in divine order through people and incidents you had no clue existed. Too, when you are fully committed to Him, God will place people in your path who you can spiritually relate to, you can help change and be changed by, and will allow you to personally grow as well as assist in you moving away from the level you have been stagnated on for so long. I am a firm believer that having an unyielding relationship with God is similar to experiencing Heaven on Earth. God always gives us glimpses of His glory and mercy. For this reason, we don't have to look far, but it is vital that we to look up beyond ourselves.

HIGHLIGHT NEGATIVE ENERGY AND EXECUTE IT

I want you to pay very close attention to everything written within the remaining section of this chapter. Highlighting and destroying everything unproductive within your personal circle that has out lived its purpose is chief in terms of moving from *Poverty to Prosperity*. Within what I consider to be the examination process towards prosperity, there are *three* vital steps in which you must take that will assist you in the decoding and re-evaluating process of the people you associate with—the people you either need to add, delete, or keep within your life. Again, it is highly imperative that you promptly begin your separation process away from what I call "Negative Energy", because we have a tendency to think exactly like those around us.

Understand, too, that the people who you identify as friends and the type of lifestyle you live will reinforce the attitude you enclose. One must be extremely careful not to feed the famished appetite of poverty.

"Do not be deceived.
Bad company corrupts good morals."
1 Corinthians 15:33

The following is a simple three step practice which will allow you to extensively examine the individuals who may or may not be good for you, in terms of you reaching prosperity, and who also do not provide you with any positive motivation or energy.

Step 1. Draw a large circle on a piece of paper with dots inside the circle. Each dot represents the people who are very close in relationship to you. These are people who you interact with, speak to, and come in contact with on a daily basis, such as your family members, spouse, girlfriend, boyfriend, casual friends, co-workers etc.

Step 2. Evaluate each of these individuals through negative and positive categorization. Ask yourself questions such as, within in my relationship with this person or people, am I moving towards God or away from God? Are they self-motivated? Do they want more out of life than I do? Are they willing to make sacrifices to progress in life? Do they motivate me to do well? Are they always complaining every time they open their mouths? Five to ten years from now, will I be able to benefit from them, and will they be able to benefit from me? In the past year have they progressed in any way? For example, have they become SPIRITU-ALLY STRENGTHENED? You will know if they have, because they will use this strength to uplift and motivate you. Have they received a promotion at work for exemplifying productive work habits, completely paid off any debts, furthered their education, started a business, or quit smoking? If you can answer "yes" to the questions that are positive then chances are those are the individuals who you need to keep within your social circle. In contrast, if you answer the negative questions with "yes", that is a concrete indication that he, she, or they are part of the reason that you are not moving forward and being productive. Notice I said, "Part of the reason." It may sound as if I'm placing the blame on someone else, but that's not the case.

Step 3. Immediately after you complete **Step 2**, diligently begin to devise a strategic plan, one which will immediately filter those individuals who fit into negative categories away from your life. Notice I did not say, "Take your time in impelling negative energy away from you." I understand, too, that some of the negative energy within your life you may consider yourself to be in love with, emotionally attached to, and entertaining for the sake of it being convenient, but you <u>must</u> undress all of the heavy items that you are currently carrying, because where you are going, that luggage will not be needed any longer. Those people or material items in which you love so much are the same elements that have you mentally and physically exhausted and at a standstill in life. You must first identify the barriers that are keeping you from executing your plan of action before you can move past them, and now that you have identified them, it's time to go! Negative energy is a powerful element and it saturates you and everyone within its path. Therefore, change what needs to be changed in your life and not what's easy.

Before I severed NEGATIVE ENERGY I

- *Tried to elude God's will for my life*
- *Decreased my reading and meditation time*
- *Wanted to enjoy the success of others*
- *Placed less focus on what I needed to be doing and more on what I wasn't doing*
- *Attached myself to excuses*
- *Settled into meticulous jobs and relationships*
- *Talked about furthering my education*
- *Made a "To Do List" and never did anything on it*
- *Lethargically sought financial freedom*
- *Appended to rejection from friends and family*
- *Waited for someone to tell me that I am on the right path*

After I severed NEGATIVE ENERGY I

- *Freely Excepted God's will and his assignment for my life*
- *Graduated from a HBCU (NCCU) with a Degree in English Literature and Writing*
- *Obtained a certification from UNC Pembroke with a GPA of 4.0*

- *Obtained a certification from Appalachian State University with a GPA of 4.0*
- *Obtained a Masters in Ameliorated English Language with a GPA of 3.8*
- *Detached myself away from excuses*
- *Detached myself away from frail friendships*
- *Desired to be surrounded by only positive people*
- *No longer desired to enjoy the success of others*
- *Gladly welcomed and embraced hardships*
- *Diligently sought financial freedom*
- *Relinquished meticulous relationships*

QUIZ 16

- In terms of moving away from or discontinuing habitual actions that hinder personal success, how important is the role of one's faith? Answer with precision.

  _____
  _____
  _____
  _____

- The following are deposits of negative energy: complainers, fear, underminers, past hurts, and joy stealers. How can you arm and protect yourself from these harmful sediments? Answer with precision.

  _____
  _____
  _____
  _____

- If possessing "Faith" means taking the first step, is it safe to assume that *blacks* within low-income environments have relinquished their rights to what God has placed before them?

  _____

  _____

  _____

  _____

- Is it at all possible for a *black* man or woman to survive America without the following: "Faith", education, sound communication and personal skills, and firm morals? Out of each tool listed, which is the most vital for one to obtain? Answer with precision.

  _____

  _____

  _____

  _____

- In terms of you reaching prosperity, what are sound motives that have kept you from prospering? Answer with precision and be as honest as possible.

  _____

  _____

  _____

  _____

17

BLACK SUCCESS <u>MUST</u> BE RECYCLED

For most people, success is defined by obtaining lots and lots of money. Society has somehow conditioned the masses into believing that a large amount of money is something one must obtain in order to be successful, which in reality is not true at all. I'm not handing over the message that having money is a wayward feature by any means; the line of reasoning in which I'm making here is that money is not the only element that defines or measures an individual's success. Success can be someone receiving an acceptance letter to a college, getting a drivers license, or even something as simple as changing a flat tire, alone, on their car for the first time. With success comes knowledge and once we become knowledgeable in a particular area, it's imperative we enlighten someone else. Unfortunately, a large number of *blacks* succeed in life and then develop self-centered attitudes. As a result, they disconnect themselves away from those who are not as educated as they may be, those who they believe are no longer on their level, in terms of goals, those who do not make as much money as they do, and those whose notoriety is not as strong as they would prefer it to be, even if these individuals are not presenting themselves as cormorants inflated with "Negative Energy".

QUIZ 17

- **Is this a natural human action?**

  _____

  _____

  _____

  _____

- **Is functioning in this manner admissible for _blacks_ who did not have anything growing up as a child or should being poor growing up be even more of a motive to remain humble?**

  _____

  _____

  _____

  _____

- **At what point do we feel like those who are less educated or not on our level professionally, even though they have not settled for living an idled life, can no longer relate to us?**

  _____

  _____

  _____

  _____

- **Is adopting this type of arrogant attitude valid in order to protect everything you have worked so hard for and earned?**

  _____

  _____

  _____

  _____

- **Is it possible to be acclaimed (famous) or very successful and still associate or communicate with the people you knew before your success, at least those who have moved away from routines you did in high school?**

  _____

  _____

  _____

  _____

I have several friends who have escaped the grips of America's ghetto politics and found success on various levels. They range from professional athletes, actors, entertainers, lawyers, university instructors, and entrepreneurs. On several occasions, I have heard taxing stories from mutual friends in regards to some of these individuals acting as if they didn't know or have anything in common with them when they crossed paths. I can honestly say that my rapport with all of these friends today, even after they have flirted with success, has genuinely remained the same. Personally, I have never had an issue with any of these individuals who have navigated their way through America's racial curfew. I sometimes wonder if it is, because I have always been known to be a very humble person and these friends of mine are all aware of the fact that I am fully conscious of their former times, which situates the certainty that they could never swell beyond humility in my eyes—or if it is chiefly, because I have obtained success on various levels and these friends view me as a prestigious status emblem who would be able to perforate the same *black* tie affair as them. Either way, I see these friends as young *black* individuals who have made a conscious decision to be different and follow whatever dreams or opportunities they desired in order to defeat grave statistics.

A major down fall, though, one that I believe we (*blacks*) have unremittingly fallen victim to, is the fact that we have become dangerously caught up in comparing ourselves and our achievements, in relation to the areas we have succeeded in, to others through a range of methods: non-tangible materialistic items, the kind of cars we drive, the clothes we wear, and the strength of our bank accounts. Exercising this demise is a hefty contributing factor to why a great deal of *blacks*, after their pompous chase of fame, lights, glamour, glitter, and gold is over, are conceiving selfish ambitions, only experiencing prosperity temporarily, and spending the rest of their lives living in major debt. It almost seems as if a large number of us (*blacks*) have forgotten the premise behind escaping our introductory tormented environments. This epidemic is unfortunate and the afflictions caused by this plague are continuously crippling *black* communities as well as the *black* race. The *black* wealth gap, in particular, is at its largest margin in comparison to our counter-parts and part of the reason for this scourge is the fact that a large number of *blacks* who are resourcefully stout are not establishing wealth for future generations, but instead are finding ways to cling to their monetary earnings, fearing they will lose their place on the social scale. I suggest that these particular brothers and sisters expeditiously revolutionize their mindsets and become fundamentally useful by helping those who are in need of financial and wealth building educational strategies. The best place to begin is with family members who are flirting with disparities and living within impoverished environments, instead of pretending not see the elephant in the room.

One becoming successful and just moving on with their life without giving back to the communities in which they come from, or any *black* community for that matter, only demonstrates self-centered diverged views of the state of *black* poverty-stricken environments. Is it safe to assume that those who fall under this umbrella have been disconnected from their roots and are afraid to get their hands dirty by getting involved with poverty issues, or were they always just selfish people to begin with? I have to raise these important questions as well. Would *Black History* be greatly affected if Harriet Tubman would have taken on this selfish attitude? Do you believe that any of those slaves who were liberally less fortunate than Ms. Tubman, once she escaped, would have been able to experience freedom if it were not for her unselfishness and wholehearted devotion to help set them free? Ms. Tubman sincerely believed she had been called by God to help her people, and while being interviewed once she said, "Now do you suppose he wanted me to do this just for a day or a week? No! The Lord who told me to take care of my people meant me to do it just so long as I live, and so I do what he told me to do."

"As iron sharpens iron, so one man sharpens another." Proverbs 27:17

This is the same devotion successful *blacks*, today, should have in their hearts for less fortunate *blacks* to help set them free from their tribulations that enslave them.

I deem successful *blacks* should offer themselves and their success as substantiation of what *blacks* can do when they incorporate discipline and hard work into their work ethic, despite where they come from. When I was younger, I was told two things by an older family member who always reminded me that humility is a very vigorous tool in life. Those two advisements where to never forget where I come from, because that's what will keep me focused when I do become successful, and if I were to ever lose focus, the same people I see going up will be the very same people I would see coming down. When *blacks* attain some degree of success, male or female, that is an opportune time to become a leader, especially within an environment that is in desperate need of tangible role models. A sobering reality is that *blacks* who have acquired success, aloft social status in America, wealth, and higher education, and correspond with the "I got mine, get yours" class, have somehow forgotten that as they brandish this means of philosophy, they are still considered to be nothing less than the (N) word in the eyes of white society. Confirmation proving this ideology to be accurate is found in the 2009 booking and disorderly conduct detainment of African American historian and Harvard Scholar Henry Louis Gates Jr., who was thought to have been breaking into his own Cambridge, Massachusetts home after Gates and his driver struggled with a jammed front door. In this particular incident, although a leading scholar in African American literature and heritage at one of the most prestigious universities in America, because of the color of his skin, all of the personal accolades in which he possess where considered irrelevant and Mr. Gates was considered an intruder first and a homeowner second in the midst of his white neighbors.

This certainty, as well, has been perpetuated within America through various media outlets, chiefly the big screen and literary works. In a 2011 article written by the Joseph S. Atha Professor of Humanities at Stanford University, Shelley Fisher Fishkin entitled *The Words of Pap Finn's Rant*, she underscored a revolting actuality that is still present today via a passage from Mark Twain's *Huckleberry Finn*. Through Pap Finn, Twain delivered a racial tirade which advocated that the white alcoholic and child abuser is enraged that a well educated *black* man had multiple liberties when he should have, indeed, been placed on the auction block to be sold:

> There was a free nigger there from Ohio—a mulatter, most as white as a white man. He had the whitest shirt on you ever see, too . . . . They said he was a p'fessor in a college, and could talk all kinds of languages, and knowed everything. And that ain't the wust. They said he could VOTE when he was at home. Well, that let me out. Thinks I, what is the country a-coming to? It was 'lection day, and I was just about to go and vote myself if I warn't too drunk to get there; but when they told me there was a State in this country where they'd let that nigger vote, I drawed out. I says I'll never vote agin . . . And to see the cool way of that nigger—why, he wouldn't a give me the road if I hadn't shoved him out o' the way. I says to the people, why ain't this nigger put up at auction and sold?—that's what I want to know.

Twain's passage is palpable confirmation that the (N) word personifies white America's trademark of unattractiveness and has been, as well, a perpetual unyielding tool to undercut the achievement of *blacks* in America. Fisher, too, agreed that it is the robust perseverance of racism within America which continues to make the (N) word in *Huckleberry Finn* a dilemma in the classroom today.

Likewise, in a speech given nearly four decades ago, Malcolm X made this same observation. While orating he asked his audience, "What does a white man call a *black* man with a PhD?" Malcolm answered, "A nigger with a PhD." Though, when he spoke of well-educated *blacks* being niggers, Malcolm X was not suggesting that education customized *blacks* into coons and bucs or anything remotely close to the (N) word; he was merely highlighting what white society thought of *blacks* during that time.

In making this point, I am reminded of a movie scene that also mirrors exactly what the white world, yesterday and today, thinks of *blacks* who carry an attitude of excessive arrogance and self-importance. This scene is from the 1971 movie, *Brother John*, which starred Sidney Poitier playing the role of a gentleman by the name of John Kane. Within this movie, you will find that the same racial conception is evident as you watch an overzealous and racist white sheriff's deputy attempt to extort and intimidate John's brother-in-law, a middle class *black* man by the name of Frank Gabriel, in the midst of a labor strike where he worked. When his attempt failed, in a furious manner, the sheriff told Frank, "You could be replaced by any Nigger that has a strong back and a weak mind." I have no intuition, at all, of the assertion(s) that possibly shaped the director's racial judgments, but what I am sure of is the fact that the dialogue within this particular scene is another repositioning reminder to all *blacks* that art (even if it is injected with racial overtones) is only an imitation of real life.

As I stated earlier, by no means am I implying that my successful *black* brothers and sisters today are anything distantly close to the (N) word. What I am unveiling and highlighting before you is the reality of the world we live within—via an unyielding memoir. And this reality advises that the white world, whether through the arts or reality, finds it to be utterly important to continually remind us (*blacks*) that we are, at least in their eyes, permanently trapped within a slave-type arrangement no matter how high our personal accomplishments ascend us through America's social statuses, no matter how successful we are or will become. And along with that point, you must understand, too, that obtaining personal success and not helping someone else ascertain the next level is dreadful and exactly what our counter-parts desire for us to do. Another sobering reality is that the same brothers and sisters who are successful and taking on this selfish attitude all come from nothing; so of all people, they specifically know what it feels like to scuffle with poverty. Many of them grew up in the same underprivileged vicinities and around the very same people they reject today.

I am a firm believer that when someone flees the grasps of destitution, they should never return with the intentions of establishing themselves as a part of what that locality has to offer, but instead, return on a mission to help someone else escape captivity. By the time my mother moved away from the projects, I was old enough to know and understand the requirements that one had to meet in order to occupy one of those government issued units. Since then, I solemnly promised myself that if it were God's will, I would never go back with the intentions of being a resident, but return only to lend a hand to someone in some form or fashion.

Today, I make a conscious effort to provide my time and service to those within the same less fortunate population that I once was a member of, every opportunity I get. I've grown to understand their meticulous plights and feelings of hopelessness, because brothers and sisters today are experiencing far more afflictions within residential housing environments than my family and I ever did. When I make mention of successful *blacks*, I am referring to professional athletes, politicians, professors and teachers, actors and successful business owners, who all have the capability to formulate a major impact in this fight against crime and poverty. We do not have to wait on the government to save our communities any longer. There are more than enough successful *blacks* who possess the means to assist in the effort to help begin the resuscitation process of struggling *blacks*. Low-income communities are in desperate need of structured after school programs and literacy centers, which need to be built directly within the low-income communities. Schools within low-income communities, whether they are private, charter, or public are all in need of books, desks, and other supplies that are scarce. I fail to understand why more of the *black* financially elite have not merged together to provide low-income *blacks* with better academic and economical options. One approach would be the opening of *black* owned banks. These would be banks for all and sundry, but more specifically those who desperately need to be financially resuscitated, educated on credit worthiness, and were deprived of financial assistance by the mainstream banking facilities that cunningly practice institutional racism. Alternatively, I am aware that there are successful *blacks* who are active in their former communities and have and are still giving back, but the number is very slim. For those who are, please continue to support low-income *black* communities by providing them with educational resources, self-encouragement, and your social support.

I challenge all *blacks* who reside within, at least, a 10 mile radius of a poverty stricken area and have the ability and resources to reach out and give back to help someone who is less fortunate and willing to be helped, as well as help them set goals and reach a plateau that will allow them to have a new outlook on life through honesty and hard work. I feel as though we should be in the "hood" with the energy of a recruiter of a fortune 500 company, searching for individuals in pursuit of a better life, because as the old proverb goes, "The journey of a thousand miles begins with one step." Once again, I have full understanding of the fact that not everyone is going to be in line with this type of assistance, but one out of an entire population is growth and progress. That's one less person who will end up in a gang, jail, or premature grave.

The majority of most successful *blacks* did not become successful on their own anyway. A great deal of them had someone to extend a helping hand in some form or fashion which, surely, assisted in them being able to reach the plateau where they are now. With this in mind, adjourn to the forefront of your thoughts the fact that not all people in the ghetto want to be there. There are scores of brothers and sisters who simply were not able to receive the opportunities that those who are successful received. Many of them had unfortunate mishaps which brutally deferred and derailed their hopes and dreams, but a large number only need one opportunity that will allow them to obtain mental liberation, academic, and financial victory. Others only need someone to just hear them out, possibly offer some sound advice, and try understanding what they are going through on a daily basis. This is a surefire method that will incontestably motivate a great deal of the low-income population to want to enhance themselves, because they can relate to tangible success.

Just imagine if all of the *black* rappers, entertainers, and athletes who have received GED's went back to the educational institutions in the ghettos where they're from periodically and personally motivated those students who always somehow register for classes but quit before the semester is over. The graduation rates would sky rocket over night, all because of a small amount of time invested into a population by someone the majority of the ghetto can relate to.

In an April 10, 2010 interview, posted on *Keepittrill. com*, rap phenomenon and multimillionaire Nasir Jones, who dropped out of school in the 8th grade, trading the classroom for the street lifestyle of his sadistic Queens Bridge locality, spoke on his decision to return to school to get his GED and the importance of having an education. Nas stated, "I am going to get my high school diploma and I want 100 men from every state in the United States to go back to school with me, young or old, who stopped going to school." He continued, "It's very important. I think that can make a difference somehow." Can you imagine how many men, after seeing this interview, were inspired and took the initiative to pursue their GED's?

Also, if local African American attorneys, teachers, and law enforcement officers within America's inner-cities would share their own success stories at urban community town hall meetings and development centers, this too would be positive reinforcement for the population. All of these *black* professionals could use their positions to reach, motivate, encourage, and establish positive and personal relationships with high risk males and females within their localities. It's very well possible that *blacks* living within low-income environments would attempt to seek self-stimulus if they knew that someone of prestige, especially someone who resembles them and escaped poverty as well, was holding them accountable for their actions. There is an immense probability they would want to prove themselves worthy and disengage away from criminal activity.

Again, I realize that this will not solve every issue within every ghetto community, but it is one of many steps that could improve each less fortunate population's confidence in the locals who are successful; moreover, this would make individuals who are products of "hood" life feel as if they are a part of a team and that their wellbeing is important to those who have made it. I ultimately believe that this would drastically help reduce the crime rate and violence that is wounding America's inner-cities. It is heartrending to know that there is an incalculable number of successful *blacks* who possess the, "If I got mine, you can get yours mentality". That's such a damaging attitude to carry, because they possess the power to help save so many lives and possibly help save the same individual(s) who could one day be carjacking, robbing, or attempting to inflict physical harm upon them while functioning in the "I gotta survive by any means necessary" mode.

As I mentioned earlier, successful brothers and sisters with this type of arrogant attitude have somehow forgotten that, at some point in their lives, someone gave them a key opportunity which allowed them to prove themselves worthy. Everyone who's made it, at some point, has received some degree of assistance that created the one opportunity needed to gain leverage and align themselves with success. There are a select few who have just done everything on their own.

In reference to giving back, this deed can be carried out in numerous methods; but of all the contributions that successful *blacks* can give an ailing low-income community, personal time is the most valuable and inexpensive entity, when recycled back into the ghetto, that will undeniably have an enormous impact on at least one individual for the rest of their life. This act will speak volumes about *black* life in America and soon cause the strongholds that *blacks* are firmly embracing to collapse from their own weight. Only then will the *black* race, as a unit, be able to rise from the ashes of rebellion to occupy its proper place in the world.

> *"Prosperity is a result of living a*
> *productive life"*
> *-Anonymous*

Everything in which I have notated methodically highlights what I feel is necessary that we (*blacks*) need to do as individuals and collectively as a race to improve the value of our lives. Highlighting problematic issues which are plaguing our race is not, at all, saying that the only problems in which *blacks* have in the United States are the ones that are happening within our culture and in each individual's personal environment. There are an uncountable number of man-made issues that are precluding *blacks* outside of our personal worlds, but this book was deliberately written to be less disturbed with those exterior contingencies that sting and oppose us, so that we can immediately begin to concentrate more on the personal changes that need to be made within our own lives. It's now been long enough that we have wasted time by lying dormant in our self-made infirmaries, suffering from our self-inflicted wounds, which is the consequence of our lack of faith in God, self-defeated attitudes, envy of one another, and fear of change. As a result, we have been using those same two mangy and broken crutches, **(crutch 1)** the race card and **(crutch 2)** excuses, trying to remain mobile within a society that unremittingly rejects us, but they are useless and no longer assisting us in transitioning to the destination where we should be.

No longer can we continue to spiritually collapse from the weight of lack of faith and surrender our lives to all of the self-sedating ideologies metropolitan avenues divulge as self-fulfilling prophesies. *No longer* can we authorize society to persuade us to go against the vision of obtaining true equality and everything that we have a right to. *No longer* can *black* men and women continue to live out the negative typecasts in which society wants them to and play into the snares which are purposely laid out for the entire race as a catalyst to continue filling detention centers, state prisons, federal penitentiaries, and grave yards. *No longer* can we continue to reject education and not use it as an essential tool to escape poverty and mental slavery, nor can we continue to practice disastrous habits which are leaving our children uneducated and illiterate—even though this country is ok with it. We have to take measures into our own hands, right now, and take this move from *Poverty to Prosperity* personal.

Ultimately, I would like to conclude this oration with an uplifting observation—one that I profoundly know in my heart is true in relation to everyone who makes up the African American race. There is no excuse why we are not pressing forward and escaping the traps, malevolent voices, and vices, in addition to the stereotypes, that our ancestors just could not sidestep. For decades we have endured financial, envious, self-hatred, and victimization burdens which have hindered us long enough. Chiefly because there is far more freedom today for us (*blacks*) to become and accomplish whatever it is we want to do, we have to begin, right now, structuring a concrete plan—at least a lone idea capable enough of leading us down a path that will eventually merge with prosperity. And while on this path, remember brothers and sisters that God loves you exceedingly and He has ordained us all to prosper just as He has any other race; therefore, through His blessings, we are entitled to personal success, a sense of self-worth, nice cars, abundant finances, sound relationships, and new homes, but be mindful of the fact that we have to be good stewards over those blessings. It's time now that we detach our minds away from impoverished thinking as well as impoverished living, relinquish hatred and harsh feelings towards those who may have hurt us in the past, execute selfish behaviors, along with feelings of insecurity and envy, and begin embracing our self-worth as well as one another, so that we can claim the prosperity that is rightfully ours. I wish all of you magnitudes of success and may your journeys from *Poverty to Prosperity* be full of blessings. God bless you all brothers and sisters. Satta Massangana.

Post Reading Examination

- In your own words, define the term "Culture". After you have written a definition, answer the following question: It is obvious that the *black* race is involved in a culture struggle. What are some strategies we must begin to implement within the *black* culture in order for a high ratio of *blacks* to begin making a transition to prosperity?

  _____

  _____

  _____

  _____

- I mentioned early that the only way to close a gap is to stand in it. Mentioning this, *black* students attending "Title I" schools who have robust reading, writing, and math deficiencies are watching their white peers from their side of the broken bridge, which are their homes. What can be done to bridge the gap between home and school to help *black* students achieve? Answer with precision.

  _____

  _____

_____

_____

- *Black* males have been set up to fail extensively in America. School systems have given up on them, mainstream society has disconnected away from them, and as a result, prison systems are welcoming them. What would you suggest needs to be done immediately to counter this state of crisis? Answer with precision.

_____

_____

_____

_____

- Although America has evolved and made strides in reference to race relations, it still has not connected with the plight of the oppressed minorities within it. Mentioning this, do you feel that there is a subtle sense of resentment towards whites by all *blacks* due to this phenomenon? Answer with precision.

_____

_____

_____

_____

- Harriet Tubman once said, "I freed a thousand slaves; I would have freed a thousand more if I was able to convince them that they were in fact slaves." With regards to *blacks* moving from *Poverty to Prosperity* today, what do the words that Harriet Tubman spoke suggest that *blacks* need to do? Answer with precision.

_____

_____

_____

_____

About the Author

Charles J. Jones is an instructor of Advanced English and Research Methods at George Mason University. As well, Jones is a column writer and motivational orator—focusing on numerous anxieties within *black* society and the education arena. He attended North Carolina Central University where he earned an undergraduate degree in English Literature and Writing. Jones continued his educational journey receiving graduate certifications from the University of North Carolina at Pembroke, Appalachian State University, and graduating with honors with a postgraduate degree in English Language Learner from Ashford University in Clinton, Iowa.

CPSIA information can be obtained
at www.ICGtesting.com
Printed in the USA
BVHW041145160523
664251BV00006B/112